GOD'S HAND IS STILL OUTSTRETCHED

Deloise Russell

Diligence Publishing Company
Bloomfield, New Jersey

The Scripture in this book is from the King James Version and the New International Version.

GOD'S HAND IS STILL OUTSTRETCHED

Copyright © 2019 Deloise Russell
c/o Diligence Publishing Company
P.O. Box 2476
Bloomfield, New Jersey

All Rights Reserved

No part of this book may be reproduced in any form without the written permission from the publisher except for brief passages included in a review.

To contact Pastor Deloise Russell to preach or speak at your church, organization, seminar or conference email: lawrence.allen1@gmail.com

GOD'S HAND IS STILL OUTSTRETCHED

ISBN: 978-0-9727416-4-4

Printed in the United States

TABLE OF CONTENTS

DEDICATION 9
ACKNOWLEDGEMENTS 11
PASTOR DELOISE RUSSELL AND ELDER 13
REWRITE THE SCRIPT 15
TO MY NEW ZION REVIVAL TEMPLE CHURCH FAMILY AND FRIENDS 16
REMEMBER YOU ARE THE CHIP! 17
JESUS WAS THERE ALL THE TIME! 18
IS THERE ANYTHING TOO HARD FOR GOD? NO, NO, NO, NO, NO! 19
ENCOURAGEMENT FOR THE NEW YEAR 19
KEEP LOOKING WITH GREAT EXPECTATIONS 20
OUR FATHER...OUR SHEPHERD 22
AMEND YOUR WAYS 23
TOTALLY COMMITTED 24
A MOTHER'S DAY MESSAGE 24
SAINTS, THOU ART LOOSED! 26
HAPPY FATHER'S DAY 27
SATAN DESIRES TO SIFT YOU LIKE WHEAT! 28
A NEW YEAR 28
WOMEN OF WORSHIP – WOW 29
FAITH IS THE SUBSTANCE OF THINGS HOPED FOR 31
NO OTHER NAME! 32
GOD'S COMMAND! 33
CHRIST JESUS IS BORN! 35

ARE YOU THERE YET????	36
STAY CONNECTED TO THE VINE!	37
NEW YEAR	37
YOU MUST KNOW JESUS!	38
SALVATION IS FOR THE REST OF YOUR LIFE!	39
THANKSGIVING	40
OUR PLAN!	41
WE ARE WINNERS AND OVERCOMERS!	43
SERVE THE LORD WITH GLADNESS!	44
TAKE YOUR STAND!	45
ALL WE NEED IS A TOUCH!	46
UNDERSTAND THE IMPORTANCE OF SERVING GOD!	47
DO YOU KNOW HIM?	48
LOVE IS A SPLENDID THING!	49
YES, JESUS LOVES US!	50
IT'S PERSONAL! YOU ARE COMPLETE IN CHRIST!	52
HOW WILL YOU LEAVE OUT OF HERE?	53
PRESS TOWARD THE MARK!	54
LOVE GOD; LET EVERYTHING ELSE GO!	55
IT DOES MATTER HOW YOU WALK!	57
FATHER'S DAY	57
DROPPED BUT LIFTED!	58
ANOTHER YEAR: I AM SO GREATEFUL!	59
LORD, IT'S YOUR TIME!	60
THE LORD MAKES US ONE!	61

KEEP YOUR HOUSE IN ORDER!	62
STAY IN THE SECRET PLACE OF THE MOST HIGH GOD	63
THANKSGIVING	63
YOUR TIME!	65
WATCH NIGHT MESSAGE	66
TEND TO YOUR OWN GARDEN!	67
THE POTTER'S TOUCH!	68
DON'T STOP PRESSING!	70
CELEBRATE!	71
EVEN NOW!	72
LOVE JESUS	73
AND WE SHALL CALL HIS NAME, JESUS!	74
PREPARING FOR THE BEGINNING OF A NEW YEAR	76
HAPPY NEW YEAR!	77
CALL TO WORSHIP!	78
HOW EXCELLENT IS HIS NAME!	79
JUST DO IT!	81
LET HIM FIX IT	82
THE WORD OF GOD SHALL ABIDE AND STAND	83
DON'T GIVE UP…LOOK AGAIN!	84
HIDE ME	85
CONTINUE IN THE FAITH	86
REMEMBER JOY IS STRENGTH	87
JESUS IS OUR SOLID ROCK!	88
WATCH GOD	90

TAKE HEED	91
TRUST AND BELIEVE GOD!	92
FOCUS…STAY FOCUSED	93
NEW SEASON	94
KEEP THE DEVIL UNARMED	95
UPON THIS ROCK	97
HAPPY RESURRECTION SUNDAY	98
FINISHED WORK	99
ON ASSIGNMENT!	101
STOP, LOOK AND LISTEN!	102
SOME WILL, SOME WON'T – WHAT WILL YOU DO?	103
GOD DOES NOT CHANGE, BUT HE CHANGES US!	104
YOU HAVE SET YOURSELF UP FOR A BLESSING	106
NOW FAITH	107
PRESS FORWARD	108
YOU MUST BELIEVE AND SPEAK NOW	109
WHAT A MIGHTY GOD WE SERVE!	110
LOVE YOUR LIFE IN JESUS CHRIST	111
JESUS PAID THE PRICE	112
ORDER OUR STEPS IN YOUR WORD!	113
WORK WHILE IT'S DAY IN YOUR LIFE!	114
HIDE US JESUS!	115
OUR GOD, OUR DELIVERER!	116
PRAISE IS WHAT WE DO	117
WALK IN THE LIGHT	118

WORSHIP THE LORD	119
RISE AND PUT ON STRENGTH	120
OUR KING IS COMING	122
OUR SAVIOR LIVES	123
JOY COMES IN THE MORNING	124
NOW FAITH IS THE SUBSTANCE OF THINGS HOPED FOR	125
REMEMBER	126
BUILD UPON THE ROCK	127
CHRIST IS THE ANSWER	128
JESUS IS TRUTH	129
GIVE GOD THE GLORY	130
FAITH – USE WHAT YOU GOT	131
FROM EVERLASTING TO EVERLASTING	132
PRAISE YE THE LORD	133
SERVE THE LORD ALWAYS	134
THE BLOOD	135
GET READY…BE READY…STAY READY	136
BY HIS STRIPES, I AM HEALED	137
A MESSAGE FROM THE SAINTS OF NEW ZION	138
THIS IS WHY! – TO YOU ALL	139
ABOUT THE AUTHOR	141
ORDER INFORMATION	143

DEDICATION

This book is dedicated to Almighty God, who gave me the inspiration through the years to write this book.

I also dedicate this work to my husband, Elder Brad Russell, my children, my family and my New Zion Revival Temple Church family.

ACKNOWLEDGEMENTS

I first would like to thank my Heavenly Father and the Holy Spirit for inspiring me to write through the years.

I would also like to thank everyone that transcribed and proofread my writings each week including Sister Patricia Wilkins, Sister Alexis Burks, Evangelist Barbara Ricks, Sister Regina Covington, and Sister Lorraine White-Garretson. My prayer is that God would bless each of you abundantly.

I am so grateful for my husband, Elder Brad Russell for always encouraging me.

I send many thanks to Apostle Gennie Holt. I remember the day I told her of my desire to write a book. She looked at some of the writings in our church bulletin and said "Pastor, you already have your book started." It was through her insight and vision that I was able to understand and see the concept for this book. She introduced me to Pastor Rebecca Simmons, who facilitated this project to completion. I pray that the Almighty God will bless you with the desires of your heart!

I would also like to thank my son, Lawrence, who has helped me with each phase of this book's writing process. May God continue to bless you and your family.

I thank Cynthia Harrell for always encouraging me to write.

Last but not least, I say thank you to my New Zion Revival Temple Church family for sparking my creativity, and for being receptive to what God gives me to write. I pray that your best gets better, and remember your best is yet to come!

If there is anyone that I did not mention by name, please charge it to my head and not my heart. Please know that I love each and every one of you.

PASTOR DELOISE RUSSELL AND ELDER

REWRITE THE SCRIPT

God's amazing grace gives us enough ink in our seemingly empty pen.
God's amazing grace will resurrect our torn life and build us up within.
God's amazing grace will show up when we are drowning in hopeless tears.
God's grace can calm our fears, doesn't matter how many years.
God's amazing grace will lift us up where we belong.
Breathe new life in us and give us a brand-new song.
Yes, God's Grace can strengthen us from the inside out.
Give us what it takes and show us what it's all about.
Like Jeremiah of old who had many trials and tests,
Declared in himself I can't take anymore. I must rest.
But God began to speak to His servant.
Jeremiah came to himself and became more fervent.
Jeremiah said my mouth is like the pen of a ready writer.
No more will I stop and become the more quieter.
Jeremiah said the presence of the Lord won't leave me alone.
For His Spirit is like fire shut up in my bones.
So get up come to yourself.

Get your hopes and dreams off the shelf.
I say to you child of God, get a grip!
And like Jeremiah, you too can rewrite the script.

TO MY NEW ZION REVIVAL TEMPLE CHURCH FAMILY AND FRIENDS

(Written for my 15th Pastoral Anniversary, June 15, 1995 and now written to you *all* through this book).

You are a jewel and indeed a most special treasure. It has been an honor and a pleasure to be your minister. Through the years I've witnessed your growth, maturity, and life-changing experiences.

Friends and relatives were able to see the work which was wrought by the power of God in your lives. Therefore, you were able to compel them to come hear the word and grow also as you have grown.

Not only is it my mission to see you grow, but it is also the mission of all our ministers to teach and minister to you. I'm thankful to God for His amazing grace, which is sufficient for me. I also thank my natural family and spiritual family for respecting the office that I hold. It has not been easy, but it is a blessing and a pleasure to paint the way through preaching the gospel. Thank you for your monetary gifts and double thanks for your love and encouragement. May God ever bless and keep you in the center of His most perfect will.

Saints, please remember one another in prayer and continue to fight the good fight of faith; lay hold on to eternal life for your best will get better and your best is yet to come. Elder Russell says the steps of a good man and a good woman have been ordered by the Lord!

REMEMBER YOU ARE THE CHIP!

Praise the Lord people of the most high God. We are blessed to meet as the church each week in the name of Jesus Christ our Lord and Savior.

Saints, God will bless you and continue to make Himself known to you through His spoken and written Word. Jesus told Peter, "...upon this rock I will build my church." Make no mistake Saints, we are the church. We are 'chips' off of that Rock. At every opportunity we must show off God's praises.

We must remember that it does matter how we act in all that we do. As the strong, we must bear the infirmities of the weak. We are each a friend of God, and He is counting on each and every one of us to build His church.

We thank God that our Lord and Savior has watched over and guided us. I remind you that you don't have to pray down fire on a potential enemy but pray down mercy.

Always remember that when it comes to your services in God's house, your labor is not in vain.

Elder always says "our steps have been ordered by the Lord." I remind you that your best will get better, but your best is yet to come. Fight the good fight of faith and lay hold onto eternal life.

JESUS WAS THERE ALL THE TIME!

The Lord, our God has blessed us again to see another day. The time He has given us, use it wisely. I remember at this time the message from Sister Ricks preached at our church one Sunday, "The 3 Rs."

God came to reconcile, restore, and renew us. It is so pleasant to dwell with Christ and stay in love and unity with one another. Resurrection Sunday is to be remembered at all times. Christ feels our burdens, feels our pain, and He will meet every need. Saints, we are unique because God made us that way. Sometimes we feel forsaken, alone and abandoned. It seems as if we don't fit in. Remember, we are unique. God loved us so much that He will withhold no good thing from us.

Thank God for Jesus Christ who loves us unconditionally, and every day He sends His Word to heal us and strengthen us. It is only you that can testify that He, your true love, has come along. One of the things He requires is that we honor Him and love Him. Always cast all of your burdens and cares on Him. Don't carry it, because the burden is too heavy; cast it all on Him.

Saints, we have been given tools for our survival; we have been given prayer, praise and worship. Use them! Remember that he who hath part in the first resurrection is going back with Christ.

Remember to fast; pray one for many many another. Take all of your cares and concerns to Jesus and believe Him.to work it out. Cast your cares upon Him for He careth for us!!

Saints, fight the good fight of faith, lay hold on to eternal life for your best will get better, but your best is yet to come. My husband, Elder Russell always says the steps of a good man and a good woman have been ordered by the Lord!

IS THERE ANYTHING TOO HARD FOR GOD? NO, NO, NO, NO, NO!

(Encouragement for The New Year)

Saints, God bless you and always keep you in the center of His will. If we are faithful to Him, He will be faithful to us. We are His people. We are the sheep of His pasture. One of the things the Lord requires is that we remain faithful to Him.

Saints, we are swiftly approaching the close of the year. Before the closing of this year, the Lord is going to answer prayers that you thought He had forgotten. The Lord, because of our faith, is going to grant some awesome victories. He is going to loose; he is going to set free. He is going to let people know He is God. So don't let go of your faith. The Lord is near, and He is very much alive. fasten your seatbelts, we are going on a ride of faith. Eyes have not seen, nor the ears have heard the things the Lord has prepared for us.

God bless everybody for your work in the house of the Lord. those who are committed to a special work and those of you who come to be in house of the Lord. Continue to pray one for another!

Saints remember to fight the good fight of faith and lay hold onto eternal life, for the best will get better and your best is yet to come. Elder Russell often reminds us that the steps of a good man and a good woman have been ordered by the Lord.

KEEP LOOKING WITH GREAT EXPECTATIONS

May the peace of Almighty God, always be yours. Peace is a fruit that will keep you walking and talking faith. When our peace is disturbed, we can so easily lose focus. Jesus said He will give us His peace not as the world gives, but the peace He gives allows us to remain strong and have good courage as we journey through here. Peace will keep us with a song in our hearts and praise on our lips. I want you to see where peace is a blessed fruit. Don't stop until you possess the fruit of peace.

Saints, our Heavenly Father loved us so much that while we were yet sinners and sinning, He sent Jesus Christ to die on the cross. God saw the fiery pit that we were headed for that is a penalty for sin; and without a deliverer to stand in our place, we would be doomed. Our Father in His great mercy and great love sent us Jesus Christ to save us. Don't give up. The way is paved. The price was paid. So don't ever give up. Keep looking up Saints, because He is always looking down on us. Don't forget to pray for one another. Keep looking up with great expectations. Let your faith cause you to look again and don't stop until your mission is accomplished.

Don't forget to fight the good fight of faith, lay hold onto eternal life, for the best will get better and your best is yet to come. Elder Russell claims and proclaims the steps of a good man and good woman have been ordered by the Lord!

OUR FATHER...OUR SHEPHERD

Saints, God Bless you. We are blessed. We are better than blessed. The Lord is our Shepherd and He will always watch over us and keep us each and every day. What a mighty God we serve! He is the source of our supply. Oh, how He loves us!

Where would we be without our redeemer; Our Savior, Our Lord, Our Father. Thank God that He stopped by Calvary to defeat Satan, death, Hell, and the grave. He rose up after He was crucified with all power in His hand. Saints, what more could He do? He told us to believe and our faith would make us whole.

Saints, lift up your heads and the King of glory shall come in! When He comes in, He will fix months and years of agony in a few minutes. So, keep on believing. Keep faith in Almighty God, for He will show up with healing in His wings.

I'm recalling now the message brought by Evangelist Ricks one Sunday at our church concerning *Signs*. They are everywhere. All signs can lead to scriptural direction if we take heed. God will bless us to overcome and be victorious Saints. Our Father is always sending a Word for us to empower us. Signs are everywhere.

Saints, continue to pray for one another, and walk in the love of Jesus Christ. God bless everyone for their work in the house of God. God will pay what is right! So, work while it is day, for when night comes, none of us can work.

Saints, fight the good fight of faith and lay hold onto eternal life, for the best will get better and your best is yet to come. Elder Russell says the steps of a good man and a good woman, have been ordered by the Lord!

AMEND YOUR WAYS

Praise the Lord, people of God. Thanks be to Almighty God who gives us the victory through our Lord and Savior, Jesus Christ. We are people who have a purpose and a reason to serve and magnify the Almighty.

Saints, in this awesome season we must be forceful in our approach to withstanding the tricks and traps of Satan. You must never forget he is cunning and wicked, and he is looking for people that he can use to do his demonic work in their lives. For those who are taught the Word and have a relationship with the Lord, Satan's mission is to get us off course, steal our joy, and make us give up our faith. Satan knows what the Lord cannot tolerate. Saints, we are not left to Satan's web; the Lord has made a way of escape for His children.

Jesus Christ was in the world in sinful flesh, and He sends His Word through the mouths of His servants, and His messengers must be as wise as the serpent and harmless as doves.

The Lord told us to cry loud and spare not, to lift up our voices like a trumpet in Zion to show

His people their transgressions. The servants must do what we are called to do in the Word, with much love, much care, and without discrimination. It is the Lord who searches the heart and tries the reins. The Word does have our answers. Saints remember what the Word says, at the name of Jesus, every knee must bow and every tongue must confess that Jesus Christ is Lord, to the glory of God the father (*Philippians 2:10-11*). Saints always hear the voice of God and answer His call with an answer to please Him.

Remember, from the pulpit to the last pew, to love, love, love out of a pure heart; be gentle and kind hearted to one another, especially as you see the day approaching.

Saints, remember to fight the good fight of faith and lay hold onto eternal life, for the best will get better and your best is yet to come. Elder says our steps have been ordered by the Lord!

TOTALLY COMMITTED

(A Mother's Day Message)

Lord, we will begin by saying how excellent you are. You have made all of us better than blessed. You have made us a little lower than your angels.

Some have not come into the knowledge that you reign supreme; but as we totally commit ourselves to you, the more our eyes open to the fact that we are nothing without you. Lord O' Lord, keep revealing yourself to us, help us with our hearts in repentance and continue to saturate us with your love. You are our Shepherd, and we are your sheep.

While man has set aside this day to honor mothers, you showed a perfect example when you left your mother in the hands of the disciple and commanded him to take care of her; To all of the mothers, happy Mother's Day. To every woman who has stood up to be a mother to the motherless, you have filled some large shoes. God bless you. To every woman with large shoulders, open arms, and big hearts that lets no child go unloved or alone, happy Mother's Day, women of God.

Saints, we serve a God who owns this whole wide world. If your season has not come, keep praising God for it is on its way. Until you see your dreams come to pass, keep praising and serving God. All He is doing is moving some stones, bricks, and mountains out of your way because straight ahead is only victory. God bless you, God keep you in the name of Jesus Christ our Lord and Savior. Continue to pray for one another; remember to · keep your eye on Jesus. Looking any other way, Satan will only show imperfection in each other. Continue to love for love covers a multitude of sins and faults. Stay focused.

Saints, fight the good fight of faith, lay hold onto eternal life for your best will get better, and your best is yet to come. Elder Russell says that the steps of a good man and a good woman have been ordered by the Lord!

SAINTS, THOU ART LOOSED!

God bless you once again. It is so good to see you walking in victory. As the sons and daughter of God, there is nothing that can come upon us if we keep the faith. If we Walk in love with praises in our mouth and forgiveness in our hearts, we will be unbeatable. Walking contrary will only cause us to start over again and again. So why start over when you can continuously walk in victory? The Lord has given us everything that pertains to life and godliness. It is in the Book.

People of God, we are in our birthing season. Tell the Lord your plans and desires in Him and He will empower you to do His will. We are in a season of celebrating Jesus' death and His resurrection. So get prepared to work while it is. day. Don't let His sacrifice be in vain. Be glad, be joyful, and most of all, be thankful that we have Christ in our lives.

Sister Ricks spoke one Sunday at our church on "The Crippled Woman." What a wonderful message. Each one of us in attendance could relate to what she said. Saints it is now your time to make your way out of your bound and crippled conditions. As Jesus spoke to that woman, "Woman, thou art loosed...," we too have been loosed. We must walk in our freedom.

To each worker in the church, what is right God will pay. In your work, He will give you blessings and in your giving, He will give you increase. God bless those who obey in their giving; you have 100% increase coming back to you.

Saints continue the good fight of faith. Lay hold onto eternal life for our best will get better, but the very best is yet to come. Elder Russell says the steps of a good man and a good woman have been ordered by the Lord.

HAPPY FATHER'S DAY

God bless you Saints of the most high God. Once again the Lord has kept us to see another day. We are so grateful. God is good and His mercy is forever. The Lord keeps revealing Himself to us. Help us Lord with our hearts and minds to receive your unconditional love.

Saints, set your sights and your focus on God. We come for no other reason but to see Jesus! We must press through and over; crawl if we must. Pastor Harris' message that was preached at our church entitled, "I've Got to Get to Jesus" reminded us that the woman with the issue of blood pressed to touch the hem of His garment; and immediately her issue was no more. Saints we must press with whatever the issue may be to see Jesus. We know that, as we press our way to

Jesus, we too will be of good comfort. Our faith will make us whole.

Happy Father's Day to our fathers. We salute every father who has been a father to the fatherless. Your broad shoulders and hearts of love do not go unnoticed by the heavenly Father.

Saints, we have been given the tools for survival, prayer, praise and worship. We just have to use them without ceasing.

People of God, fight the good fight of faith, lay hold on to eternal life, for the best will get better and your best is yet to come. Elder Russell reminds us again that the steps of a good man and a good woman have been ordered by the Lord!

SATAN DESIRES TO SIFT YOU LIKE WHEAT!

(A New Year)

God bless you Saints. Praise God for another glorious day. In all of our lives, what Satan has meant for evil God has turned it around. We are coming into a brand-new year. God has started some things in the past year, and He is continuing in the new year. God wants us to head to a new level in our walk with Him. We have seen Satan busy. We must be more about our Father's concerns. We must pray more, fast more, and get into the Word more to stand with our armor on ready for battle. The weapons are not carnal, but they are mighty through God for pulling down Satan's strongholds. God chose us for such a time as this. What a mighty God we serve!

People of God, whatever you do; keep your faith in God through Jesus Christ, our Lord! We are in a time now when the redeemed of the Lord must say so! It is not what we see but it is what we believe! We must be like Queen Esther. She said, *"If I perish, I perish but I am going to see the King!"* What she meant was, nobody will stop me from getting to my destination. We must have the same mindset and tenacity. If you do not come fully persuaded, then Satan can knock you off. Stay full of the Holy Spirit because God's grace is sufficient!

Saints continue the good fight of faith. Lay hold onto eternal life for our best will get better, but the very best is yet to come. Elder Russell says the stcps of a good man and a good woman have been ordered by the Lord.

WOMEN OF WORSHIP – WOW

Praise the Lord people of God. We celebrate women who have put their hands to the plough and never gave up. No matter what the struggle was, women have always put God first in the name of Jesus. A wise woman knows that without God we can do nothing.

People of God, we must remember the struggle and say WOW. Nobody but God could touch the heart of willing workers; whether standing with men of God, marching with the masses, or preaching on the floor of many churches (because we were banned from the pulpit), none of these things moved us. We pressed through in the name of Jesus and we were elevated by our heavenly Father. We still cooked, we still were wives, we were mothers, and still in the ministry. The world can now see women in the church have arrived. God cannot be left out of our plans. It is God who made all of us, called all of us and gave us an assignment to usher in His return.

In Christ Jesus, there is neither male nor female, we are people of God doing the work of God. Lifting up the name of Jesus in a dying world, living holy, walking in grace and integrity, keeping our heads up, and praising God every day for victory and freedom.

To God be the glory for all He has done in the name of Jesus Christ. WOW be strong in the Lord.

People of God, fight the good fight of faith, lay hold onto eternal life, your best will get better, but your very best is yet to come! Elder Russell says, our steps have been ordered by the Lord!

FAITH IS THE SUBSTANCE OF THINGS HOPED FOR

Saints of God, be of good cheer and always trust in the Word of God. Sometimes it seems as if trusting and believing His Word is so hard for us to do. Whatever you do, don't stop taking God at His Word because there's a blessing coming your way. God dealt to each of us the measure of faith and told us how to use it. In great expectation of receiving your blessing, continue to serve God and have faith in Him.

We are blessed to know that we're kept by the faith of God, and we'll continue by that same faith. We must be determined to lean on and totally depend upon Almighty God. We should not have any confidence in the flesh.

Saints, pray without ceasing. Always look to Jesus, who is the author and finisher of your faith. Aren't you excited about your faith? If not, you need to be in a hurry to get excited because your miracle is on the way. Some miracles are right around the corner and others are just outside the door. Remember when your testing times come, your motto should be "God is my deliverer, God is my shelter, and God is my very present help in the time of need."

Saints, God has begun a good work in us, and He will perfect everything concerning us. So while we're still on earth, let us serve the Lord with gladness and come before His presence with thanksgiving. Continue to be encouraged. Don't give up, and most of all, be determined about your faith in God knowing that He will see you through. Remember to love Him with all of your heart.

Saints, keep working while it is day. When night comes, no one can work. Continue to put in your time because your payday is coming.

People of God, fight the good fight of faith. Lay hold onto eternal life. Your best will get better, but your very best is yet to come! Elder Russell says, our steps have been ordered by the Lord!

NO OTHER NAME!

People of God, greetings in the name which is above every name, Jesus Christ! When this precious name is called, every knee must bow, and every tongue confess that Jesus Christ is Lord. He is the ruler of the universe, the Savior of the world and as a matter of fact, He is the first and the last. There is no other way to get to God the Father except through Jesus Christ, the Son, the one who became flesh, who took our sins, paid the price for our sins, and set us totally free. All we have to do is accept Jesus Christ as Lord and Savior.

Saints, we are living in an exciting time for the church. It is good to be saved at a time like this. Many people are seeking the Lord as never before. People are beginning to see that there is no other way to live. Those who have been in the race for so many years, don't stop now. We must remain in the arch of safety, Outside is sinking sand.

Saints, the Lord has sent His Word to heal, strengthen, empower, and always to encourage us. There is no sin or temptation that Jesus Christ didn't die for. Don't think it strange when Satan gets more vicious. Don't fear because we have been given power over the devil. We are winners!

Remember Saints to pray without ceasing. Don't stop praying! You must stop fretting, worrying, and having anxiety attacks; and be still in your spirit, your faith, and your walk with Christ. Let nothing move you from the hope of the Gospel.

Continue to fight the good fight of faith. Lay hold onto eternal life. Our best will get better, but our very best is yet to come. Elder Russell says that our steps have been ordered by the Lord!

GOD'S COMMAND!

God bless you again Saints of God. I greet you in the name of Jesus Christ, our Lord, who died, rose, and is alive forevermore. We enter into the service of God each week to offer up sacrifices of praise with the fruit of our lips.

Don't think it strange when some enter the house of God running, clapping, crying and shouting because God is working quick miracles or answering longtime prayers. What we see and hear are Saints taking the time to bless the Lord for what He has done. God is yet restoring families, giving peace and restoring us. Saints who have asked ·and believed with thanksgiving will get a blessing from the Lord which will' be more than enough for an overflow.

Saints, there is a place for us to get to that is commanded by Almighty God. We have been: called to this place; It is a place of surrender, sanctification, and holiness. It is a place of letting go of everything that's not like Christ and the things that are an abomination to Him. It is a place of saying not my will, but Thine will be done!

As soon as we head to the commanded place in God, the place of total obedience, we'll have joy unspeakable full of glory. No test or trial can separate us from God in the commanded place. When we get to that place, God will be able to trust us. Saints, the signs are upon us and the handwriting is on the wall, we need to get to the commanded place! Hurry, pray, fast, and surrender.

God be with you Saints is always my prayer.

Keep fighting the good fight of faith, lay hold on to eternal life; your best will get better, but your very best (Jesus) is yet to come. Elder says, our good steps are ordered by the Lord.

CHRIST JESUS IS BORN!

Praise the Lord saints of the living God. It is again a privilege to write and encourage you to be strong, courageous, and to hold on to your faith. Buckle up for a rough ride and know our Lord and Savior was born to take our sins away. To everyone who believes, God has given us power to become children of the Most High. Our Deliverer, our Redeemer, God is with us and He promised never to leave us.

People of God, our Lord and Savior Jesus Christ was born to die. The prophets of old spoke of a king being born to deliver His people. Well, He was born. Some still don't believe, but those who believe keep the faith, receive the new birth, and endure as a Christian until the end. What a glorious end it will be!

This is a season of celebration to every child of God, a season of thanksgiving, a season of knowing our Jesus is still alive, and we can call Him every day forever until He calls us home. With everything going on in this world we are happy in our souls knowing our eternal salvation is settled. Jesus is coming back again! If you don't know Him, ask Jesus to come into your heart and forgive your sins, and He will. Your new life will begin.

People of God, fight the good fight of faith, lay hold on to eternal life, your best will get better, but your very best (Jesus) is yet to come. Elder

Russell says, don't forget our good steps have been ordered by the Lord.

ARE YOU THERE YET????

Praise the Lord Saints. God bless you, keep you, empower you and prosper you. As I pray that you are blessed, I pray that the body of Christ is blessed. As we are strengthened in faith and excelling in His love, we know that the grace of God extended to us has made us rich in Him. We are in a position now to be strengthened in all things in Christ.

Be wise Saints because this is the time. Don't think the enemy is asleep! Be watchful as you continue your work. Saints, know what the will of God is concerning you. For each of us, God's will in our life is that we remain "faithful." Don't lose hope, don't be distracted, stay focused and keep your eyes on the prize! Doors will be opened, ways will be made, and we will be better than blessed!

Saints, we have seen the Lord's work many times, Satan's job is to make us disbelieve that God is working on our behalf. Remember Satan is a liar! The Lord gives us survival tools. You will survive! – As long as you know the "Chief Shepherd" is going to appear, and when He shows up everything will be worked out. That is why it is so important to keep the faith, keep serving God, and keep looking up. Our faith will make us whole!

I thank each of you who show up for weekly church services. I thank God for those who sing for us, usher for us, and all who serve in God's house. We haven't arrived yet Saints but we are on our way. We are closer than we want to believe.

Continue to fight the good fight of faith. Lay hold on to eternal life. Your best will get better, but you very best is yet to come. Elder reminds us that the steps of every good man and good woman have been ordered by the Lord!

STAY CONNECTED TO THE VINE!

(New Year)

Dear Saints, God bless you. Our new year has begun. Our Lord, God is still on the throne! He has given us all of the things that pertain to life and godliness. What a new time, what a new beginning; a time to go forward forgetting those things that are behind. We have been given a new chance to be stronger, more focused, more faithful and more focused on serving the Lord.

Remember to keep your hope and faith alive. This is our new season. Let this new season allow us to trust God more, to love more and have the determination not to be tricked or trapped by the devil; because he is still the devil. We are obligated to stay connected to the vine according to John 15; draw a line and not let the devil pull us across that line. That invisible line will always let us be reminded that we don't cross onto Satan's side to weaken us. We have the victory! Our blessing is on the horizon. We are going to be more blessed. Whatever you need, thank God in advance, keep working in the house of God. Remain faithful, stay prayerful, stay in your Word, and let God! This is a time of abundance. Abundance in faith, peace, joy, and finances.

Continue to fight the good fight of faith. Lay hold on to eternal life. Your best will get better, but you very best is yet to come. Elder reminds us that our steps have been ordered by the Lord!

YOU MUST KNOW JESUS!

God bless you Saints of the most high God. He is good and His mercy is forever. While we spiritually walk through our past and into our future, we can truly say it is God all of the way. As we look over the past weeks, we have noticed turmoil all over our country. Satan's actions have been vicious, but I have some good news for you. don't fret because Jesus is the answer for the whole wide world. Those of us who know Jesus must not let go of His unchanging hand.

Saints, every day that we wake up is a blessing. Don't take it lightly. God sent us some wonderful, powerful words through the Holy Spirit for our learning, obedience, and sharing.

Our obedience will bring us victory and blessings. We will be able to speak victory to each situation that faces us. Our faith will follow, and we will have unspeakable joy and glory.

Whatever you do, please don't stop working for the Lord because everything will come to a halt, and only what you do for Christ will last.

Saints, continue to look to the hills where your help comes from – our Lord God who made heaven and earth. Let us continue to pray and love one another.

Continue to fight the good fight of faith. Lay hold onto eternal life. Your best will get better, but your very best is yet to come. Elder Russell says, the steps of a good man and a good woman have been ordered by the Lord!

SALVATION IS FOR THE REST OF YOUR LIFE!

God bless you Saints of the most high God. The Lord has blessed us with another opportunity to praise His holy name. We are God's chosen people. Since we are God's children, we must take on His characteristics and be like our Father.

Saints, we must not forget that our crosses are never too heavy to carry. We have an advocate with the Father. When the devil comes to discourage us, we must remember that "God's got it." Remember the power that comes forth when we plead the blood of Jesus. Let nothing separate you from the love of our God! Our Father in His great mercy and great love sent us Jesus Christ to save us. Don't give up. The way is paved, and the price is paid. Don't ever give up!

Saints continue to pray without ceasing. We must continue to hold each other up in prayer. When we have the God kind of love for our brothers and sisters, we will always include them in our prayers.

Fight the good fight of faith, lay hold onto eternal life, for your best will get better, but your very best is yet to come. Elder Russell says, the steps of a good man and a good woman have been ordered by the Lord!

THANKSGIVING

God bless you people of God. We are in a time set aside by the world to give thanks on a special day, Thanksgiving. But to the Saints, we know that every day is a day of thanksgiving. We thank God from the rising of the sun until it goes down. We have so much to thank our God for, so don't let a day go by where you forget to bless and thank God.

Saints, think of the times during this year when you didn't know how you were going to make it or when disappointments would cease. But in every dilemma, our heavenly Father showed up and made everything all right. Although the Lord will avenge us of our troubles, we must remember that Satan still wants to sift every one of us like wheat.

Each time anything comes up in our lives, it will take faith to bring us through. Faith is so essential in our walk with Christ that Jesus Christ has prayed that our faith does not fail us. When He returns, He wants to find faith at work on earth and in His children.

Many thanks Saints for all of your work and your labor. It is God's laborers that keep things moving in His house. There are not enough thanks or enough pay that can show how much your work in Christ is appreciated. Thank you so much for the prayers for the sick, shut in, and bereaved.

People of God, fight the good fight of faith. Lay hold onto eternal life. Our best will get better, but our very best is yet to come. Elder Russell says the steps of a good man and a good woman, have been ordered by the Lord!

OUR PLAN!

God bless you people of the most high God. Build your hope on nothing but the precious blood of Jesus! When Jesus died on the cross, a new revelation began. Pathways opened to all people to get honor from the God of heaven. At the cross

Jesus' death, burial, and resurrection gave us a seat in His kingdom. An assurance policy that if we die, we shall live again. A hope that goes beyond the grave, and a life in Him that guarantees we are one with the Father, Son, and Holy Ghost. ·

Saints of God, we really need to keep digging deeper in the Word. We will always come up with a strength that whatever comes against us, whatever the devil has planned for our hurt and destruction, will always backfire. All we need to do is stick to the plan the Lord has laid for us. Jesus made us winners before the foundation of the world. Through time God sent His Son, Jesus, who gave His life. God always brings to our spirit that He will supply all of our needs according to His riches in glory by Christ Jesus. So stand fast in Jesus Christ and let nothing separate you from His love. Jesus is the best plan that ever happened to us!

Remember Saints, you are warriors! Don't forget to pray! Let your desire be to get closer to God. Desire God. Desire Him with your whole heart and everything will fall into place. Love the Lord God with all of your heart is the message for the church, for everyone, desire God with your whole heart.

Saints, fight the good fight of faith. Lay hold onto eternal life. Our best will get better, but our very best is yet to come. Elder Russell said, he cannot say it enough, our good steps have been ordered by the Lord!

WE ARE WINNERS AND OVERCOMERS!

Praise the Lord people of Almighty God. Our Lord is an awesome God! In the name of Jesus Christ, our Lord has made us winners, and overcomers, and He keeps doing great things for us. As we lift us our heads, our King of Glory will come in.

Saints keep the faith. Have faith in God. He will take you through any problems, setbacks, and setups you might encounter in this walk with Jesus. Don't let His Word slip out of your heart. The devil fights the Christian to steal the Word through heaviness and weariness. Since the Lord has made us winners and overcomers, your instructions come from the Word of God. You must read, study, and keep the Word in your heart! As we eat our breakfast, lunch and dinner to maintain our physical bodies, our spiritual food is necessary.

People of God, fight the good fight of faith, lay hold on eternal life. Let nothing separate you from the Word and the will of God. Our best will get better, but our very best is yet to come. Continue to pray for each other. Elder Russell says our good steps are ordered by the Lord!

SERVE THE LORD WITH GLADNESS!

God bless you people of God! It is my hope and prayer that you are blessed above and beyond your greatest dreams. I pray that your love and devotion for our heavenly Father through Jesus Christ always lets you look at one another through the eyes of love. The love that Jesus has given His children leaves us with compassion, pity, and prayers for all mankind that they might recover themselves from the snares of the devil; he is already defeated. We are the overcomers, we are the righteousness of God in Christ Jesus. All we have to do is set our affections on things above, not the things of this earth.

People of God, ignore the devil. He is always trying to get our undivided attention, just ignore him. Keep praising, keep blessing, and ALWAYS Keep believing! Saints, know without a shadow of a doubt, our God rules supreme. Continue to pray for those who have lost loved ones in this hour. Pray for the household of faith.

Church of the living God, stand on the promises of God, not leaning to your own understanding, but acknowledging our Savior in all things!

Continue to fight the good fight of faith, lay hold on to eternal life; your best will get better, but your very best is yet to come. Elder says, indeed ALL of our steps are ordered by the Lord.

TAKE YOUR STAND!

Saints of God, bless the Lord from where all blessings flow!

Take your stand in Him as the three Hebrew boys did, as Daniel did, and all of the saints after them. There comes a time in your life when if you are on the Lord's side, you must declare it in words, deeds, and actions. Even in the midst of all your discouragement, downfalls, and pitfalls, take a stand for Christ! Sanctify yourself! Let Him sanctify you holy!

Saints, we are in a time where we cannot play the blame game. We cannot continue to blame family, friends, circumstances, situations or hurts we have been through. In spite of all of these things, the Lord will keep us and take care of us. We must ask Him to hide us until these troubles pass. He will do just that!

Saints there are so many things happening today; terrible things, pitiful things, and to the world, hopeless things. But we the church know like Job that we have a change coming.

Continue to fight the good fight of faith. Lay hold on to eternal life. Your best will get better, but your very best is yet to come. Elder reminds us that the steps of every good man and good woman have been ordered by the Lord!

ALL WE NEED IS A TOUCH!

Praise God for another week, a new month coming, and for this season. We are a blessed people and the Lord really continues to do great things for us.

In this new year, the move of God has started. Those who keep the faith, will do mighty things. Every message we have heard has been designed to increase our faith, strengthen our walk, and admonish us to set our affections above; not on things of the earth!

Remember the messages that you heard in church each Sunday. They are blessed Words. Take heed. Saints, I have great expectations and hopes for you. Without Christ it will not be possible. Pray without ceasing! When the Lord touches us, He changes everything. He takes away our disappointments, our headaches, physical and spiritual hurts, and unforgiveness. We begin our walk in pleasing Him. All we really need is a touch from Jesus, and He gives us a bunch of love.

Thank you, Saints, for your work in the Lord and the upkeep of God's House.

Continue to fight the good fight of faith and lay hold on to eternal life. Our best days will get better, but the very best is yet to come. Elder says the step of a good man and a good woman have been ordered by the Lord!

UNDERSTAND THE IMPORTANCE OF SERVING GOD!

God bless and keep you from day to day, this is my prayer for the body of Christ. When our Shepherd keeps our house, He will always lead us to safety·.

I want to impress upon you the importance of staying connected to our power source. That power source is the Father, the Son, and the Holy Ghost. In Him we live, we move, and we have our being. When we choose not to stay and live every day connected, dedicated, and happy in Jesus Christ, we have left off the part, the plan, and the purpose that will successfully keep us on course of our spiritually connected, holy fulfilled, and satisfied life while on this planet earth.

We cannot in this body serve two masters! Serve the Lord with gladness and know, without a doubt, He is God and besides Him there is room for no other. Love the Lord, your God with all of your life. Our spiritual life prepares us for our eternal life.

People of God, fight the good fight of faith. Lay hold onto eternal. life, your best will get better but your very best is yet to come. Elder Russell says, remember church that our good steps have been ordered by the Lord.

DO YOU KNOW HIM?

Saints, we are the people who are supposed to love the Lord with all of our hearts at all times. There is no reason with the resources we have been given, with the new covenant we have been given to allow the devil to rob us of our joy. This is the season that the Lord has shown Himself strong, mighty, and powerful. Through all of our storms, He has given us the victory. The scripture says, the weapons of our warfare are not carnal but mighty through God that gives us the ability to pull down strongholds *(2 Corinthians 10:4).* I remind you again, weapons may form but they will not prosper!

Saints, I challenge you to go on a five day fast and bombard heaven with praises and thanksgiving. Whenever you think about a problem, whenever you have a need, whenever a devastating situation arises, praise God! The praise will bring you out and meet your needs because it is going to be met by faith. During these five days don't ask Him for anything. Praise Him for meeting every need and for bringing you out of every pit. Use faith to strengthen your faith by believing God.

Saints, the secret is: What you have already asked for, you already have. Now, you praise Him because faith says you have it! Don't abort your blessings by beginning to think and say to God, "I asked you. You didn't do it." or when asked "How are you doing?" and you reply, "Well ahh..." Just say, "By faith I've got the victory!"

Continue to fight the good fight of faith. Lay hold onto eternal life. Your best will get better but your very best is yet to come. Elder Russell says, the steps of a good man and a good woman have been ordered by the Lord!

LOVE IS A SPLENDID THING!

People of God, it is my sincere prayer that as the days go by, we are stronger in faith, more committed to God, and more dedicated to the Word. With this life, no devil can defeat us.

Our lesson on how important it is to love out of a full heart is essential in our walk with Christ. If we don't love people, we won't be able to love God as we should. The scripture says let every person be A liar, but let God always be the truth. God said love Him first and then each other. In doing this, everyone will know that we are His disciples. As we grow in this love, we will learn to forgive quickly!

When Jesus came into Jerusalem riding on His donkey, palms and coats were thrown for Him to ride across. Shouting "Hosanna, Hosanna, blessed is He," some of those people were the same ones who shouted "Crucify Him! Crucify Him!" He was about to die to take our sins upon Himself and set us free. Jesus saw what was going to be the suffering, the pain, and the agony. He asked the Lord to let this cup pass, He saw us in the cup, (it was a bitter cup) and said, "Not my will but thou will be done."

People of God the love that He had for God's creation became a splendid thing. Nobody, nobody made Him do it. He did it just for us.

Don't forget Saints to love one another. Love is a splendid thing!

Fight the good fight of faith. Lay hold onto eternal life. Your best will get better but your very best is yet to come. Elder Russell says, the steps of a good man and a good woman have been ordered by the Lord!

YES, JESUS LOVES US!

Greetings to you in the name of our Lord and Savior, Jesus Christ. Did you stop to think today how you are really truly blessed and highly favored by the Lord? The thoughts He has towards us is to bless us and position us to successfully carry out our assignments. We can overcome every test, trial, and pitfall. There is no stumbling block that can stop us if we stay in continued fellowship with Him. In your time of prayer and communication with Him let Him know He is your very source. Do this daily! Remember, your walk with Him is by faith and not by sight.

Saints, remember to praise the Lord at all times because God through Jesus Christ, dwells in the midst of our praise. Open your spiritual eyes and see that it is why we are always tried. Through every trial, our Deliverer is standing in the midst to deliver us.

Our hiding Place is God our Father. He is our deliverer, healer, and strengthener. We must always give God praise no matter what our state is. In your walk of faith know that our Lord died for our sins, He was wounded for our transgressions. We are healed by all of His stripes!

Saints, we are in our resurrection remembrance time. What a time it is! Our Lord died and rose again for everybody who is born into this world. Our Lord gave His life so we could have life. God blessed everyone who named the name of Jesus and dedicated their life to Jesus Christ. We have such a promise from the Father through Christ who said, "1will lose not one."

Saints we are in a time of victory but if victory is not accepted, we will walk in defeat. So, wake up and walk in your deliverance. That is what His death is all about. He defeated Satan at Calvary, took back the power and declared He has all power now and whosoever believes in Him will not perish. Don't forget Revelation 19th and 20th chapters; live on this earth becoming the bride of Christ. Let your walk be by faith and not by sight. Set your eyes on Jesus.

People of God, fight the good fight of faith, and lay hold onto eternal life. Your best will get better, but your very best is yet to come. Elder Russell says, the steps of a good man and a good woman have been ordered by the Lord!

IT'S PERSONAL! YOU ARE COMPLETE IN CHRIST!

People of the most high God, mercy, grace and peace be multiplied to you through the knowledge of Jesus, our Lord. He has kept us and blessed us again to be a blessing. We must be grateful for every chance and opportunity to be in His service. Those minor setbacks are to discourage us. They are sometimes to confuse us and to ultimately end in making us faint. So use your time wisely, redeem your time wisely, and inform the devil that you will bless the Lord at all times.

Saints, this is a time of refreshing. If we look around and count up the cost, you will see that your good times always outweigh any bad times. I encourage you today to stay focused, keep your eyes on the prize, and this is Christ.

On a personal note our church, New Zion is proud of our Men's Fellowship. We encourage them, we are behind them, we are praying that God leads them, and that Elder Russell continues to be strengthened in the Lord and lead us forward. God bless each of you that are participating and continue to anoint you. Men, stay focused on your purpose.

Saints, continue to pray one for another that all of us are healed and personally fight the good fight of faith. Lay hold onto eternal life, for your best will get better, but your very best is yet to come. There is no time like the present to make your election sure! Elder Russell says that our steps have been ordered by the Lord!

HOW WILL YOU LEAVE OUT OF HERE?

Saints, God bless you. Once again we have the opportunity to praise the Lord and to lift up the name of Jesus. When we look back on our lives, we can say what a difference the Lord has made in our lives. Our heavenly Father made a way of escape for all of His children. Please take advantage of the sacrifice that Jesus made for us on the cross. Don't let the shedding of His blood be in vain. He truly did His part.

Saints, our Lord reigns supreme and His grace and mercy have been sufficient. What great love He has bestowed upon us. Always have courage and keep faith in the Lord and Savior, Jesus Christ. He will never let us down.

We must keep our eyes on the prize Saints. The prize we are striving for is life eternal. We are victorious! Always keep Jesus on your mind. Set all your affections on things above, not on things of this earth. The Lord will fight our every battle. The Lord has some wonderful things in store for those who love Him.

Our church's recent Men's Fellowship made Zion proud during their Men's Day Service. Elder Russell's message about "The Stalker" was uplifting and reminded all of us how to and why we must "behave wisely" at all times.

Saints, continue to pray one for another that all of us are healed and will personally fight the good fight of faith. Lay hold onto eternal life, for our best will get better, but our very best is yet to come. Elder Russell says, that our steps have been ordered by the Lord!

PRESS TOWARD THE MARK!

God bless you people of the most high God. We are so much better because our eyes are open, and we can see our Father as the only wise God. Many in the world have not received or accepted Him as their Lord and Savior. They have missed out on a treasure on earth.

"Lord, our Lord how excellent is thy name in all the earth! You are our Savior, our redeemer, our healer, our mind, body, and soul regulator. Nobody but You could set your captive children free."

Saints, the Lord has told us, to get into His Kingdom, we must press. Press means to push against anything that tries to keep us out of His presence. You must boldly press and don't stop. You must press with force! To the believer, it is worth the press! Saints keep trusting God. Keep His commandments. Clap your hands and remember our victory is in Christ Jesus, our Lord! Don't let go of your faith.

We thank God for another day. We wake up each morning with new grace and mercy. God bless you for your labor in His name. Always pray for one another and always for the body of Christ that we are totally healed. To workers in Zion, God bless you. No matter what your labor of love has been for the Master, what is right, He will pay. He will not forget your labor.

I recall a message preached at my church one Sunday entitled, "It has already started." Rumors of war and wars have already started. That means we must look up for our redemption is drawing near.

Saints, fight the good fight of faith, lay hold onto eternal life, for our best will get better, but our very best is yet to come. Elder Russell reminds us that our steps have been ordered by the Lord!

LOVE GOD; LET EVERYTHING ELSE GO!

Saints, may God bless you and continue to make Himself known to you through His spoken and written Word. As we read and listen to His Word, we get to know more and more of Him and how we must pattern ourselves after Him. Since we are God's children, children of the Most High, we must take on His characteristics and be like our Father.

Saints, we are a blessed and precious people. We need to write it in our hearts how God counted us as His friends so that when the devil comes to discourage us, we can remember that we are a friend of God's. Saints, can't you see how blessed we really are? We 've been kept another day, another week; another month has come to an end and we're still here to see the entrance of a new day! Whenever "things" try to hinder you, just let it go and know that God will take care of you because you are His child. Have faith in God. He'll always see about us because anything that concerns us concerns Him.

Saints, continue to pray without ceasing. We must hold each other up in prayer. When we have the God kind of love for our brothers and sisters, we will always make sure they're included in our prayer agendas.

Remember only what we do for Christ will last. God loves you.

Saints, fight the good fight of faith, lay hold onto eternal life, for our best will get better, but our very best is yet to come. Elder Russell says, the steps of a good man and woman have been ordered by the Lord!

IT DOES MATTER HOW YOU WALK!

(Father's Day)

God bless you people of God. Greetings in the name of our Lord and Savior, Jesus Christ. If you are reading this message, you are still here. Another chance, another opportunity, and another day to place your confidence and your trust in nobody but God through Jesus. He is the answer! Our Heavenly Father cares for us. No matter how bad it seems, just wait on Him. He will surely show up. Sometimes suddenly, sometimes in the last seconds; but know He will be there. Keep the faith and remain faithful.

Saints, the promises of God are sure. Sometimes we make promises and take vows; but very often circumstances and situations do not allow us to fulfill our promises. The Lord knew we were flesh and sometimes we say things and change our minds. When the Lord makes promises to us and seals it with an oath, we are consoled by the fact that God said it and it will come to pass!

God has blessed us to see another Father's Day! Congratulations to all of the Fathers. We thank God for the Fathers who have passed on. Their memories will never fade. For those who don't have an earthly Father, all of us have a heavenly Father and He loves all of His children.

Continue to fight the good fight of faith and lay hold onto eternal life. Our best will be better but our very best is yet to come! Elder Russell says that the steps of a good man and a good woman have been ordered by the Lord!

DROPPED BUT LIFTED!

Saints, it's another day and we are still here to bear witness that the Lord is wonderful, is merciful, is loving and new mercies each day have been extended to us. Many tests and many trials left us for demise, but along came Jesus and He lifted us.

Remember, this is our season; so no matter how rough it gets, our faith in God through Jesus will sustain us. No cross, no crown. We will reap in due season if we just don't faint. Failure and fainting are not options; but pressing on to our victory through praise, obedience and worship coupled with prayer will continue to bring us victory. So, no matter who or what dropped us, through our faith we are lifted!

Bless the Lord at all times and continue to labor in His house; for what is right He will pay. May God give you a hundred-fold return in all your giving and serving in His house. Saints, please remember one another in prayer.

Continue to fight the good fight of faith and lay hold onto eternal life; for your best will get better, and your best is yet to come. Elder Russell says the steps of a good man and woman have been ordered by the Lord!

ANOTHER YEAR: I AM SO GREATEFUL!

This is (was) an exceptional year. a year that the Lord has anointed us to preach good tidings unto the meek. The Lord has: sent us to bind up the broken-hearted. to preach liberty to the captives and to open the doors of the prison that many individuals are bound by.

We are on assignment. and I thank God for another year with New Zion Revival Temple. I am so grateful for so many prayer warriors and caring people. God has continued to give me a special love and deep concern for each and every one of those entrusted to my care.

Many thanks to Elder Russell. a wonderful and thoughtful husband who always wants the best for me and our children, grandchildren, and great-grands: each one name by name. Thank you Elder.

To a blessed church with anointed people who want to see the best for each other. We are blessed among millions. I thank God through Jesus Christ our Lord that He has us together. May God multiply your kindness.

Thank you to every minister. To everyone who has given prayers and financial support to my family. My prayer is that you have a one-hundred-fold return!

You pray for me as I pray for you and watch God fix it!

Saints, please remember one another in prayer, continue to. fight the good fight of faith; lay hold onto eternal life for your best will get better and your very best is yet to come. Elder Russell says that our steps have been ordered by the Lord!

LORD, IT'S YOUR TIME!

O Lord our God how excellent are your ways! We are blessed to have such a great deliverer as you. We didn't do anything to earn your dying for our salvation. But because you did, we can live.

Thanks to the Lord for He has made every provision for us to be saved. When we take steps to take inventory, we can see He left nothing out. All we have to do is fast, pray, and praise. There are things we must do for the things that are already done. As a matter of fact, it is ours for the asking. As I preached in one of the messages the Lord gave me, "...press toward the mark for the prize of the high calling of God in Christ Jesus. Press thru the pain!"

Saints, build your faith in the Word of God; sanctify yourself holy unto the Lord. It doesn't matter who doesn't or who does, just make sure YOU are in right standing with God Almighty. Press steadily!

Remember to pray for one another. Pray for those in authority, pray for the lost, and make sure you do it cheerfully.

God has allowed us to see another week. In the week coming up we want to be stronger, we want to be more blessed than we were last week.

Continue to fight the good fight of faith. Lay hold onto eternal life. Your best will get better. Your very best is yet to come! Elder Russell says, "Our steps have been ordered by the Lord!"

THE LORD MAKES US ONE!

People of God, greetings in the name of our Lord and Savior, Jesus Christ. What a week! We praise God that we made it. How blessed we are to have mercy, grace and lots of favor. These benefits are given to the people of God. Through many tests and trials, we are always victorious and undefeated. Remember we are people of purpose. We are called to show the world how the Lord meant for us to live, how to treat one another, how to face fears, overcome obstacles, and most of all how to cast all of our cares on Him. It's not just a saying. Our Savior really cares for us, He wants us to be one in Spirit.

We thank God for His Word on Women's Day Sunday at our church, "On Your Mark, Get Set, and Let's Go!" God does what God does, but you must be in the race to win it!

People of God, don't stop praying for one another. Pray that broken hearts are mended. Pray that sinners run to get saved. Pray that the saved stay saved and grow in grace.

Keep fighting the good fight of faith, and lay hold onto eternal life, for your best will get better, and your very best is yet-to come! Elder Russell says, the steps of a good man and a good woman have been ordered by the Lord!

KEEP YOUR HOUSE IN ORDER!

Saints, let us bless the name of Jesus Christ our Lord and Savior. He let us live to see another day to come together to lift up His Holy name and to offer Him our praises. He's such a loving Father who loves His children. As the days approach, we should be drawing closer to our Father, looking to Jesus who is the author and finisher of our faith. God is standing with His arms outstretched so mankind can run into them. He doesn't want any one of His children to be lost. He wants us to be saved and to stay saved.

Saints, we serve a mighty big God and we shouldn't place any limitations on Him. He is the Great "I AM." Serving Him should be our number one mission in life. Serving Him IS walking in truth. SO, take your eyes off each other and learn to love each other. You should be praying with all of your heart that your brothers and sisters reach their eternal home.

We must not be ignorant of Satan's devices, and we must always keep ourselves armed with the Word of God. Satan is petrified that we came out of the situations we were in. Don't play with Satan. He'll do all that he can to tempt us to be "out of order." It has to become personal for each of us to make up our own mind to stay on the Lord's side until we die.

Saints remember our standards are set by God. Therefore, we are trendsetters. Our righteousness must always supersede the world's. God is the only one who can give life in this dying world, and we must always lift Him up. Continue to set your affections on things above and not things on this earth.

Keep fighting the good fight of faith. Lay hold onto eternal life, for your best will get better, but your very best-is yet to come! Elder Russell says, "Our steps have been ordered by the Lord!"

STAY IN THE SECRET PLACE OF THE MOST HIGH GOD

(Thanksgiving)

Praise the Lord Saints, for our God is worthy to be praised. As we approach the Thanksgiving season, let's start now making it a point to give daily thanks for all His blessings. Our time is precious, and we shouldn't waste it. We should be fasting more, praying more and living more for God. Starting with the next breath we take, we should have a "just do it" attitude for the Lord.

Saints, it's our heavenly Father's good pleasure to give us His Kingdom. We should constantly press toward the mark and don't stop until we come into the presence of God. The more we learn of Jesus Christ and His ways, the more we should want to know. The more we know, the more power we'll have and the more victorious we are.

Remember when times get tough in your life that the darker the cloud the more powerful the rain. Those dark clouds will bring powerful rain. You are going through, and He is going to send the rain. We must be obedient to God's Word and continually strengthen our relationship with Him. Saints, continue to pray for each other. Let the Lord hear from you, then listen so you can hear from Him. It's a good thing to give thanks to the Lord. We must look for ways to please the Lord and bless His name.

Saints, continue to fight the good fight of faith. Lay hold onto eternal life, for your best will get better, but your very best is yet to come! Elder Russell says, our steps have been ordered by the Lord! Continue to pray for one another!

YOUR TIME!

Saints, remember as time goes by that we are still blessed people. I want to remind you of the times you are in. Our time now can be rough, or we can be going through good times; but what I want you to understand is that this time is the only time that you have. Good, bad, or indifferent, it is how we respond to our time.

To all who are walking according to His Word and going through a challenging time, wait on the Lord; He will constantly renew your strength. To those at this time when things seem to be working out, don't stop praying. Be an encouragement to those who seem like their time of blessing will never come. Remember, now faith is the substance of things hoped for and the evidence of things not seen.

While at this time keep praising God, for to everything there is a season.

Saints keep your hope and your faith consistently before God. Let your light shine before men so that at this time they will see your good works and glorify your Father which is in heaven. We are called for such a time as this. Those who are strong in the Lord will survive the storm. Those who are not strong in the Lord will have to be resuscitated. It is better to be strong than to faint along the way.

Continue to fight the good fight of faith. Lay hold onto eternal life, for your best will get better, but your very best is yet to come! Elder Russell says, the steps of a good man and a good woman have been ordered by the Lord! Continue to pray for one another!

WATCH NIGHT MESSAGE

Saints of God, what a year we've come through! We had many laughs, tears, disappointments and tests, but thanks be to God Almighty for bringing us through. Drying our tears and calming our fears He gave us joy to replace the heavy spirits that were on us. Last year was also a season where we had victories. Joy should overwhelm us and fill our hearts as we come into this New Year. We've been given another opportunity to be stronger in the Lord, to love Him more and to forgive all injustices done to us.

Saints, the Lord requires us to love each other as He loves us. Let this be your year to praise God more and be more determined to let NOTHING and I mean NOTHING separate you from the love of God. This is the time for us to be rich in prayer and fasting, having a great expectation that the Lord will show Himself strong in our lives. This year we're going to see many prayers answered, so don't you dare faint, lose hope, and most of all don't lose your faith in God!

We don't need to make new year's resolutions because daily we resolve to have a sight unseen, no matter what comes our way, knowledge that our God will see us through, looking to the hills for our help. Regardless of our situation, we have decided we're going to live for Jesus each and every day.

Saints, continue to pray for each other. We need each other's prayers, and our prayers surrounded by faith.

Fight the good fight of faith. Lay hold on to eternal life. Your best will get better, but your very best is yet to come. Elder Russell says to every good man and good woman, your steps have been ordered by the Lord!

TEND TO YOUR OWN GARDEN!

People of God, we are blessed to see another week go by and to look forward to the coming week. It's not that we have been so good, but it's that God is so good to us. As you go into your tomorrow, always make sure Jesus is in the forefront. Whatever we do in word, deed, or action, do in the name of Jesus. To leave Him out is a spiritual mistake.

Saints, it is so important to read, study, and assemble; our strength and continuous recovery is in the presence of God at all times. Thinking we have a handle on our life and our finances without His direction, is a mistake. How would you know what He expects if you didn't let Him tell you? I encourage you to love the Lord with all your heart, your strength and your mind. Love your neighbor as yourself, especially those of the household of faith. Walk and talk as Jesus would and do it with love.

Remember Saints, your heart is your ground. Tend to your garden. Keep your heart with diligence.

Fight the good fight of faith; lay hold onto eternal life, for your best will get better, but your very best is yet to come. Elder Russell reminds us that our steps have been ordered by the Lord!

THE POTTER'S TOUCH!

Bless you people of Almighty God. We are better than blessed because our heavenly Father brought us and kept us another week. Each day the Lord, gives us is another day to open our eyes with grateful hearts knowing that it was only God who woke us up. Nothing and no one made Him give us another day. It was His decision to let us have more time. We're here because of God's grace and mercy; therefore', we must show forth our praises redeeming the time because the days will grow evil. Our Jesus is the only one who makes days worth living.

Saints, although the days have been challenging, it's okay because Jesus told US these things would be, so don't be surprised when you're tried and tested. Just know your Father will never leave. you alone.

Remember to work while its day and keep your faith in God...'It would be impossible to please God if we try to walk this Christian walk without having faith. Regardless of what each day may bring, walk it by faith and not by sight. I've said many times· before, this is a sight unseen walk, but with God on our side, we will make it to the other side.

Therefore, we must praise God, rejoice forevermore. Love each other and love Him with all that's within us. This is God's will for His children.

The Lord came that you might have life and' have it more abundantly. So cheer up! Our Lord overcame the world and we are overcomers too! Be happy in your walk with the Master. Remember only what. We do for Christ will last. In the midst of our days of weeping ·and sorrowful hearts, always remember it's just momentary. It will pass and the sun will shine.

Saints, fight the good fight of faith, and lay hold onto eternal life, for your best will get better; but your very best is yet to come!' Elder Russell says, "The steps of a good man and a good woman have been ordered by the Lord!"

DON'T STOP PRESSING!

Saints of God be of good cheer and always trust in the Lord. Sometimes it seems as if trusting and believing His Word is so hard for us.to do. Whatever you do, don't stop taking God at His Word because there's a blessing coming your way.

God dealt to each of us the measure of faith and told-us how to use it. In great expectation of receiving your blessing, continue to serve God and have faith in Him. We are blessed to know that we're kept by the faith of God and we'll continue by that same faith. We must be determined to lean and totally depend upon the Almighty God. We shouldn't have any confidence in the flesh.

Saints, pray without ceasing. Always look to Jesus who is the author and finisher of your faith. Aren't you excited about your faith? If not, you need to be in a hurry. to get excited, because your miracle is on the way. Some miracles are right around the corner and others are just outside the door. Remember when your testing times come, your motto should be, God is my deliverer, God is my shelter and God is my very present help in the time of need."

Just as Jesus laid down His life for us, we have. to totally surrender our will to Him, or we'll become tools for the enemy's use. We're in the fight of our life, and we must be willing to let go of our will and let God have His way. Each one of us must come to the conclusion that God is God and He has to be the center of our life.

Saints, God has begun a good work in us, and He will perfect everything concerning us. So, while we're still on earth, let's serve the Lord with gladness and come before His presence with thanksgiving. Continue to be encouraged, don't give up, and most of all be determined about your faith in God; knowing that He will see you through. Remember to love Him with all of your heart!

Saints, continue to put your time in because your payday is coming. Fight the good fight of faith. Lay hold onto eternal life, for your best will get better, but your very best is yet to come! Elder Russell says, your steps have been ordered by the Lord!

CELEBRATE!

Saints, we've come to another time in our life where the Lord has blessed us once again. We've witnessed the passing of another day. While we might yet have some unanswered questions and prayers, we can rejoice because we still have life and hope. The hope that we have does not make us ashamed or afraid because our hope is in Jesus Christ. Therefore, we can keep pushing on knowing that our deliverer is on the way. So, keep your faith strong, and exercise it by praying and believing every day.

Saints, it's celebration time because of what Jesus did for us on Calvary. He was wounded, smitten and put to death so we would be alright in a time like this. We are able because Jesus did it all: He paid it all for us on Calvary.

Saints, we are reminded to get right with God. Rejoice, and in all things give thanks. This is the will of God concerning us. After you have done all, remember to pray without ceasing.

Saints, God bless you for your faithfulness to Him, to His house and to each other. Always bless the church and enter in with praises. This is the house God gave us to gather together and worship in His name. Thank you for all your sacrifices to make His name great!

Saints remember to bless the Lord at all times and let His Word always be in your mouth.

Fight the good fight of faith. Lay hold onto eternal life, for your best will get better, but your very best is yet to come! Elder Russell says, "your steps have been ordered by the Lord!"

EVEN NOW!

Saints of God, I pray that peace, God and the Holy Spirit be multiplied to you. That your growth in Christ and your obedience to His Word bring abundant rewards and much needed strength.

All of God's children have been designed to win every battle. We have an inside helper who always brings us deliverance through His Word.

People of God, the Lord is familiar with and is touched by our every infirmity; He can surely do what is needed to make sure we are victorious. We are in a season of blessings. Being in a season of blessings doesn't mean that the devil is asleep. Set your sights and your focus on what God has said. If we do that, we will never fail. Remember, even death has no dominion over us. Though we die, we shall live. If you are down, get up for even now God can and will turn it around.

Saints don't let a day go by that you don't remind the Lord of how good He is. Give Him His praises. If your praises go up, blessings will come down. God bless all that your hands do to lift His name in work in His house. What is right, He will pay. There is no other way, from here to eternity.

Saints bless the Lord at all times. Continue to fight the good fight of faith, lay hold onto eternal life; for your best will get better, but your very best is yet to come! Elder Russell says, "your steps have been ordered by the Lord!" Continue to pray for one another!

LOVE JESUS

People of God, praise the Lord. It is our God, our Lord who has given us eternal life through His blood. Our Lord gave His life that we might live! We are happy in Jesus because He let us see the plan that will bless us day by day.

Saints, walk with Jesus every day as long as you live. Our safe place is in Christ Jesus, our Lord. If you have life, you have the opportunity to be strengthened, to be righteous, and to be holy. The Lord left us His Word to show us, encourage us, and let us see and recognize that Jesus is Lord. We must be in love with Jesus. He is the author and finisher of our faith.

Saints, love the Lord your God with all of your heart, soul, mind and body. Love one another! We thank our Lord for a new day, a new year approaching, and a new time to get more strength, more power, and to submit totally to our Savior. The devil is mad with God's children because we are heaven bound!

Fight the good fight of faith; lay hold onto eternal life, for your best will get better, but your very best is yet to come. Continue to pray for one another. Elder Russell says, our steps have been ordered by the Lord!

AND WE SHALL CALL HIS NAME, JESUS!

Greetings people of God. I want you to know today is a new day, yesterday is gone, and tomorrow is 24 hours away. Bless and praise your heavenly Father who is aware of our daily struggles. He knows traps and snares have been laid for each of us to stumble and fall by the enemy of our soul, the devil. But when we call on Jesus Christ, He will guide us through every minute and every hour of the day. Read the Word of God. His Word is settled in Heaven forever. His Word is sweet like the honeycomb. When we enter into the presence of the Lord, we enter in with thanksgiving and we bless His name.

Saints, we are coming into a new season. This just might be the season that our Lord and Savior will return. "For unto us a child is born, unto us a son is given: and the government shall be upon his shoulder and his name shall be called Wonderful, Counsellor, The mighty God. The everlasting Father. The Prince of Peace." *Isaiah 9:6*

People of God, let us continue to go into the house of the Lord knowing that if it had not been for the Lord on our side, we would have fallen time and time again without hope. But, because we know Jesus, we sometimes fall down in our faith, in our walk, but our Saviour will throw us a lifeline, and He will pull us out of despair, and we will get up again. Oh, how we love Jesus!

People of God, get up, get moving, get your war clothes on and fight for your worship. Fight for your praise. Fight the good fight of faith!

Lay hold onto eternal life. For your best will get better, but your very best is Yet to come. Continue to pray. Be strong in the Lord. Elder Russell says our good steps have been ordered by the Lord!

PREPARING FOR THE BEGINNING OF A NEW YEAR

Praise the Lord saints of God, we are blessed to prepare for a new year; a new beginning. With our new year, we must put our total trust in our Lord and Saviour, Jesus Christ.

Saints, do some rebuilding. Be strong in the Lord and no matter what may come or go, keep building. Fast, pray, worship, bless the Lord, and be like Nehemiah when the enemy comes to tempt you with unhealthy thoughts and actions. Nehemiah said, "I will not come down!" What a word of faith. Again, I say rejoice!

In the book of Nehemiah, the builders were working on different parts of the wall; but each builder, because of the enemy, had their sword along with their tools. We must also, according to Ephesians 6, take the helmet of salvation, and the sword of the spirit; which is the Word of God. Our fight is not with flesh and blood, but with principalities and powers, rulers of the darkness of this world and spiritual wickedness in high places. The devil, Satan, has put his demons in places to defeat the children of God, but our Father in the name of Jesus is greater than any devil or demon that is dispatched in this world to defeat us. Pray calling on Jesus, our Deliverer.

People of God, fight the good fight of faith, lay hold onto eternal life, for your best will get better, but your very best is yet to come. Continue to pray;

be strong in the Lord. Elder Russell says, our steps have been ordered by the Lord!

HAPPY NEW YEAR!

Praise the Lord everybody, what a blessing it is to be able to praise the Lord and clap our hands to our King, our holy one, our anointed one; Jesus Christ our Lord.

People of God we have been given another season in our life to make changes for the better; A closer walk with God and a greater commitment to serve the Lord and to serve notice to Satan that our Father and Savior, Jesus Christ will be the one we will serve, praise, and worship. He is the one that has promised us and can give us eternal life. The thief has stolen enough of our tears, stolen enough of our time, and really enough of our bodies. Our Father, who made us, deserves all of our service. Our Father and Savior, Jesus Christ has made a way for us to escape a place called Hell where there is no grace, no mercy, and no forgiveness.

We choose Jesus, who died for us. Don't let another moment slip away without blessing the Lord at all times. Shut your eyes and praise the Lord for your new season, a time of abundance and restoration.

People of Zion you have remained faithful and our Father will withhold no blessing. He will continue to strengthen you on every side. All you have to do is ask.

People of God, we don't need to make New Year resolutions because daily we resolve to have a sight unseen, no matter what comes our way, faith, knowing our God will see us through. Looking to the hills for our help, we are nothing without Christ. So, regardless of our situation, we've already pre-determined we're going to live for Jesus each and every day. God bless you! It's a new season; it's a new day!

Fight the good fight of faith; lay hold on to eternal life. Your best will get better, but your very best is yet to come. Elder Russell says, the steps of a good man and a good woman have been ordered.by the LORD!

CALL TO WORSHIP!

God bless you, people of God! We have been called to worship and all of His worshipers must worship God in Spirit and in Truth. God is looking for His children to turn their hearts totally back to Him, to serve Him with gladness, to be happy to be saved, and happy to be sanctified. To be set apart, to be called out, to live holy, and to seize every moment to let the Lord know how much we appreciate what He did on Calvary's cross. He gave His life so we can be forgiven and set free from bondage to Satan. He has given us a chance to live our lives in abundance without worry and without failure.

Saints, "worship" means to offer great devotion to our Savior We can't let trouble stop us. Our trouble is just a setup for us to be blessed. We serve a mighty deliverer, what more can He do than what He has already done? We have an expected great end. While we are here, windows, doors, and miracles of all kinds will be granted to us. Serving God through Jesus Christ our Lord and Savior is the only way. Praise the Lord for our spiritual, physical, and financial blessings and they will become greater. Present your bodies as living sacrifices, holy, and acceptable unto a living God.

Saints, this is a time of abundance. Abundance is faith, peace, joy, and finances. Believe and you will receive!

Worshipers continue to fight the good fight of faith and lay hold on to eternal life. Your best will get better, but the very best is yet to come. Elder says, our good steps have been ordered by the Lord!

HOW EXCELLENT IS HIS NAME!

People of God, this is the day that the Lord has made! Don't let this day go by without rejoicing and showing how much it is appreciated. If every day was happy with no problems, no struggles, and nothing to pray about, then we would never rejoice. But people of God, we must rejoice every day because it is a day we've never seen before. It is a day full of promise and possibilities; Let your faith reach up to the Lord and trust in the Lord with your whole heart.

Saints, the Lord is our light and our salvation. He is excellent in all the earth. We are blessed to be in the family of the Almighty God! He always makes a way for His children, and He sends His Word to strengthen, heal and deliver us so that our confidence in Him will be unmovable and unshaken.

Saints, remember we have Christ Jesus on the inside of us. Cheer up! We have the greater one on the inside. Christ in us is the hope of glory. The Lord is on the inside of His believing children. Saints, work while it is day for when night comes in our life, all work will cease. May you have a financial increase, a spiritual increase, and physical increase. Work, fight, and bless the Lord at all times.

Fight the good fight of faith. Lay hold onto eternal life. Your best will get better, but your very best is yet to come. Elder Russell says, the steps of a good man and a good woman have been ordered by the Lord. ·

JUST DO IT!

Praise the Lord Saints! The Lord is always showing up and always sending His angels to do battle for us. When you need your angels, in the name of Jesus Christ, call for them.

People of God, in Jesus' name, I am reminding you that we have been given a new start. When we accept Jesus with our new start, our sins have been forgiven. Our records that were against us have been wiped clean. We have Jesus Christ on the inside, our hope of glory. We have been given a measure of faith. If we believe, we can receive and see many miracles. We can build on our most holy faith because we have been given victory over sin and Satan. We have been given a way out and a way back to God through the shed blood of Jesus! That is why Satan is so angry with God's human race, God's masterpieces, because there are none like us. We have gotten eternal life.

Saints, when you are tempted, know that the devil wants us back. So worship, praise, and don't give up; we will have a glorious finish. Eyes have not seen, and ears have not heard what the Lord, our God, has prepared for those who love Him and love Him forever until our end.

"Give thanks unto the LORD, for He is good; His love endures forever." Psalm 118:1

...give thanks unto the Lord; call upon His name; make known His deeds among the people." Psalm 105:1.

People of God, fight the good fight of faith; lay hold onto eternal life. Your best will get better, but your very best is yet to come! Elder Russell says our steps have been ordered by the Lord; mankind is his creation!

LET HIM FIX IT

Saints, have you stopped to consider how mighty our Father is? There is none like Him. He loved us so much that He put on sinful flesh and became the Word in action. He stopped by Calvary to have a day where He put His finger up and told the devil, 'I told you, you were going to get put back in your place, under the feet of the saints of Almighty God.'

Our father, in the name of Jesus, told each of us to keep the faith, don't doubt Him, walk with Him, love Him, and He would take us to the other side. No matter how bumpy the travel is, just stay connected to Him; because heaven belongs to us, but here on earth, He will keep us. Saints know and stand on the Word of God God's Word will stand and abide forevermore. At His Word things change. Let the revolution of celebration begin. Our Savior deserves the praise.

People of God, keep working for Jesus while it is daytime in our lives.

Don't forget to fight the good fight of faith and to lay hold onto eternal life. Elder Russell says that the steps of a good man and a good woman have been ordered by the Lord! Saints, we have better days coming! Even our best days will get better, but the very best is yet to come!

THE WORD OF GOD SHALL ABIDE AND STAND

People of God, praise the Lord. It is a blessing to be able to share blessings, hopes and dreams with each other and pray that each other's faith remains strong until God's desire for our lives is fulfilled. We have much to accomplish in our lifetime so that lost souls can come to know the saving grace of God through our Lord and Savior, Jesus Christ.

Saints, sometimes when we pray, answers don't seem to reach us, and disappointments are on every side. For God's sake don't stop praying and don't lose your faith. You are a faith keeper and your reward will be multiplied. When we pray, God will hear us, and He will answer! Continue to pray for each other because the devil is after us; he has no respect of persons.

He uses different strategies and approaches for different people, but his aim is to stop us from believing. The devil doesn't want us to plead the blood of Jesus on him. We must remember whose we are, rebuke him, and plead the blood when he starts up.

Saints study the Word of God so you will always know what is being said according to His Holy Word. We know that in the beginning was the Word, the Word was with God, and the Word was God! He spoke all things into existence by His Word. God's Word is POWER, LIFE and TRUTH. We must know the truth and to know the truth we must study the Word and listen to the preached Word. When you need further understanding, ask God. He will unfold His Word with clarity and give you wisdom and strength to continue the good fight of faith and to lay hold onto eternal life.

Your best will get better, but your best is yet to come. Elder Russell says that the steps of a good man and a good woman have been ordered by the Lord!

DON'T GIVE UP...LOOK AGAIN!

Praise the Lord Saints of God. The Lord's grace and mercy have been our covering. His Word has been our shield and our life.

Although we are apart from our church families during the week, we still have that connection. We are all calling on the same God who is our Father. People of God, "Do not give up." When you feel like giving up, look again because you have another miracle. You have another blessing. You have another way out and another way in. He can shut a door, and nobody can open it. He can open a door that nobody can shut! It depends on what kind of answer you need – an open door or a shut door.

Make sure you always stay in God's presence. Wherever you are, abide in Him and He will abide in you. Let nothing distract you!

Keep working for Jesus, serving Him and continue to fight the good fight of faith. Lay hold onto eternal life. Your best will get better, but your best is yet to come. Elder Russell says that the steps of a good man and a good woman have been ordered by the Lord!

HIDE ME

Saints, we serve an awesome, mighty God. He has been so good, and there is no searching of His understanding. When He created the heaven and the earth, He had no one to monitor Him, instruct Him, or rule over Him. He counseled His own self. He gave us so many wonderful things. Everything He has given us has been given to us for one purpose. We give Him praise, we give Him thanks, and we want Him to lack nothing. Every chapter in the Bible from Genesis to Revelation always points to His return. Whatever happens between the pages of our lives, is only making us fit for His Kingdom.

It has been said and demonstrated that everything in this world that we see with our eyes is only temporal. It will pass away. So, if the beauty of this world has you fascinated, it is only for us to realize that every brick and every tree, as beautiful as it is; will pass away. Set your affection on things above not on things of this earth.

Saints, this is an SOS; **S**top, **O**pen your eyes and **S**ee. Time is winding down so make your love connection, and love the Lord our God with all of your heart, mind, and soul. Love one another! Remember there is power in the name of Jesus. There is power in the blood of Jesus, and the Lord is our refuge. Our very present help in the time of calamity! Don't you dare give up Saints!

Continue to fight the good fight of faith. Lay hold onto eternal life. Your best will get better, but your best is yet to come. Elder Russell reminds us that the steps of a good man and a good woman have been ordered by the Lord!

CONTINUE IN THE FAITH

God bless you mighty people of God. Our God has shown himself to be mighty and strong in battle. He is worthy to be praised. No matter how hot the battle, we can always lean on Him. He is a strong tower and a very present help at all times.

People of God, continue to look to the hills where your help comes from. Our Father is high and lifted up. Yet He is touchable and reachable. He is just a prayer away.

Saints, I ask you to continue in the faith because if you continue, you will reach the finish line in victory. If you don't continue in the faith, you will have defeat!

So choose to fight the good fight of faith. Lay hold onto eternal life. Work while it is day. Your best will get better, but your best is yet to come. Elder Russell says that our steps have been ordered by the Lord!

REMEMBER JOY IS STRENGTH

People of God, we are in a new opportunity! Changes are taking place, things are looking up, blessings are being reaped, and hope is coming back alive. It is up to you as to how you receive it. Put 100% into your walk with Christ, and you will have a return that can't be matched. God has declared days of blessings and power. He will send His Word and change the atmosphere. The Lord has told us to go and He will go with us. He told us to speak, and He will speak for us. He said to honor Him, and He will honor us. This Is our time to believe and to receive.

Saints, the Lord requires us to love each other as He loves us. So, let this continue to be the year to praise God more and be more determined to let nothing and I mean NOTHING separate you from the love of God. This is a time for us to be rich in prayer and fasting, having great expectation that the Lord will show Himself strong in our lives·. This year we're going to see many prayers answered, so don't you dare faint or lose hope, and most of all don't lose your faith In God. When you come into the house of the Lord, set your sight on Him instead of being a busybody, a bench warmer or a judge. Come in with the attitude of gratitude and filled with the anointing of the Holy Ghost. Come in the door blessing the 'Mighty God; Our ·Great King Jesus Christ, Our Lord.

    Continue to pray for each other. We need each other's prayers, .and let your prayers be surrounded by faith.

Saints, continue to fight the good fight of faith. Lay hold onto eternal life. Your best will get better, but your best Is yet to come. Elder Russell says that the steps of a good man and a good woman have been ordered by the Lord!

JESUS IS OUR SOLID ROCK!

Saints of God, we thank our God from whom all blessings flow. He has been so good, so merciful, and so kind. There is none like Him. If we searched our lifetime, we could find none that can compare to our Lord and Savior, Jesus Christ. He has brought us from a long way in a short time. There is no god in this world that can change your life, save your soul, pull you from the pit of destruction, form you, translate you, and confirm you at the same time. Nobody but Jesus!

Anyone that is building and leaving Jesus out of the master plan has left out the pillar that holds the building together. Jesus is our foundation. He calls us to stand and weather every storm. Our Jesus has to take us where we are going. To go someplace without Him is going on a journey that will end in destruction.

Saints, remain alert, watchful and always keep your mind on Jesus. Be faithful and walk in faith. Jesus prayed that we would keep the faith. Saints, believe God, because He will see us through. When Jesus stops by your house, will He find faith? If your faith has been tried, don't you dare give up. Because God says, He swears He will bless us!

Saints, continue to fight the good fight of faith. Lay hold onto eternal life. Your best will get better, but you best is yet to come. Elder Russell reminds us that the steps of a good man and a good woman have been ordered by the Lord!

WATCH GOD

Saints, may God bless you and continue to make Himself known to you through His spoken and written Word. As we read and listen to His Word, we get to know more and more of Him and how we must pattern ourselves after Him. Since we are God's children, children of the Most High, we must take on His characteristics and be like our Father.

Saints, we are a blessed and precious people. We need to write it in our hearts how God counted us as His friends, so when the devil comes to discourage us, we can remember that we are a friend of God's. We must let nothing separate us from our God.

Saints, can't you see how blessed we really are? God will take care of us because we are His children. We must pray without ceasing. We must hold each other up in prayer. When we have the God kind of love for our brothers and sisters, then we will always make sure they are included in our prayer agendas. "Pray for me, I'll pray for you and watch God change things!"

Continue to fight the good fight of faith and lay hold onto eternal life, for the best will get better and your best is YET to come. Elder Russell says the steps of a good man and a good woman, have been ordered by the Lord!

TAKE HEED

God bless you people of God. We are better than blessed! Death, sickness, and disease has been all around us. Yet, we have lived to see another day. Do not take it for granted that you had to be here. None of us had to survive. That is why the scripture tells us to always give thanks. For this is the will of God concerning us.

Sometimes we ask the question, "What is God's will for me?" One of His greatest wills is that we would be thankful. That we would have hearts of gratitude. It is God who made us. We didn't make ourselves. When we rise up in the morning, it should be the beginning of a day of worship! All through the day, anytime of day, be grateful!

Saints, God bless your faithfulness to the house of God. Continue to love the Lord with all of your heart, mind, soul, and body. Love your neighbor as yourself. Be quick to forgive and slow to judgment. For when we forgive, we will be forgiven! What judgment we measure will be measured back to us.

Saints, don't forget to continue to fight the good fight of faith. Lay hold onto eternal life. Your best will get better, but your very best is yet to come! Elder Russell reminds us that our steps have been ordered by the Lord!

TRUST AND BELIEVE GOD!

Saints, God bless you. We are the people of the most high God. God loves us so much that while we were yet sinners, His only begotten son, walking this earth in a fleshy body died on Calvary's cross for our sins. He shed His precious blood to wash our sins away. He took the power of sin out of us and gave us a fresh start, a new start and told us He will always be with us. Don't be ignorant of Satan's devices because He defeated Satan and we can do the same thing.

Jesus gave us the power and told us we can go through in this world. All we need to do is to have faith in God, trust in God, and believe He will do what He said in His Word, which is His covenant. He told us to, praise God, bless God, and know that Jesus paid the price so we could always be overcomers. Let God through Jesus Christ be your desire. Love Him, reverence Him. If you do this, He will move Heaven and Earth on your behalf. People of God, some people will not believe Him, will not fear Him, will not obey Him and will not worship Him. But there are those who have decided to make Jesus their choice! Jesus their life! Knowing He is the way, He is the truth and He is the life. Now Saints, be about your Father's business. Don't forget to pray for one another every day during this season.

Saints, remember the house of God. Assemble yourself, worship and praise Him as we labor in the Lord. Our labor is not in vain. Ministers of the Gospel of Jesus Christ feed you the Word of God.

Bless them as they bless you. Walk in love, walk in forgiveness. Read Proverbs 6:16. There are six things God hates, the seventh is an abomination. He wants us to love one another and forgive one another. Let's do the right thing!

Saints, just know all of your labors, no matter what your role or what you have done in His name, will be rewarded and you will have His favor.

Continue to fight the good fight of faith. Lay hold onto eternal life. Your best will get better, but your very best is yet to come! Elder Russell reminds us that our steps have been ordered by the Lord!

FOCUS...STAY FOCUSED

People of God, we thank the Lord for bringing us through another day. As never before, we must keep our eye on the prize. Stay focused on the vision. Keep His Word at all times before us. When we let His Word remain in us when we are tested and when we are tried, we will always come out a winner. Saints, this is a season that we have been given where our faith will bring us through to victory.

The Lord has some breakthroughs, some blessings in store for us, and He is depending on us to keep the faith. Our faith unties His hands and He will channel blessings our way.

Saints, don't forget to fast. Fast that heavy burdens be loosed, that the hopeless receive hope, and those who are about to give up will be restored in their minds and their hearts. Fast that our families come to Christ, that the weak will become strong and that those who are away from God come back to Him and serve Him with gladness. Most of all, that for every trap that Satan has set, that we don't become ensnared! Remember what I previously said, "Don't lose your joy!" Be glad that Jesus called you. Be overjoyed that you answered the call.

Saints, keep in mind to watch over your children as they use social media on their phone and on the computer. Parents/guardians, you *can* know what they are doing. Utilize the parental controls and monitor what your child is doing. Young people, children, DO NOT GIVE ACCESS TO YOURSELF!

Continue to fight the good fight of faith. Lay hold onto eternal life. Your best will get better, but your best is yet to come. Elder Russell says the steps of every good man and good woman of God have been ordered by the Lord!

NEW SEASON

Praise the Lord people of God. We are in our new season, our prosperous season, our overflow season. Don't allow unbelievers to crowd out your season. Saints, we are so grateful to our heavenly Father for His delivering, keeping and heart-fixing power. He has kept us through the good, the bad and the ugly times of our lives. We thank God for every new day. Because every new day brings a new beginning. We lift Him up because He always brings us a victory.

It's our new season. It really is. Don't you give up your vision. Don't you give up your faith concerning your blessings. Always remind Satan what a liar he is and then tell him what a mighty God we serve. Remember there is no competition. We are winners! Hold on to the spoken words that have come across the pulpit. Hide the Word of God in your heart so you won't sin against Him.

Saints, continue to fight the good fight of faith. Lay hold onto eternal life. Your best will get better, but your best is yet to come. Elder Russell says that the steps of a good man and a good woman have been ordered by the Lord!

KEEP THE DEVIL UNARMED

Praise the Lord people of God. The Lord is still blessing us. One thing I want you to remember – The Lord is bringing in more blessings. Don't focus in on things that went wrong. God will make them right. God is making the weak strong. He is turning lack into prosperity. All He needs is your faith to believe. The Lord is our very present help.

Saints, the Lord has given us the ability through His Word to pull down strongholds. To pull them down, we must love the Lord our God with all our mind, all of our soul and present our bodies holy and acceptable unto Him. Love His Word and trust His Word, for His Word is true! Don't forget to thank God at every waking moment and all through the day. Take your eyes off of folks. Human beings are not where your help comes from. All of our help comes from God through Jesus Christ, who is our Lord!

"For the vision is yet for an appointed time, but at the end it shall speak, and not lie: though it tarry, wait for it; because it will surely come, it will not tarry." Habakkuk 2:3 KJV

Saints, I want to thank all of the workers in the ministry who did not think it was robbery to give their life to the work of Christ. Whether you are a door keeper, a floor sweeper, melody keeper, or you just show up; whatever your function in the house of God, you are an asset to the ministry. God bless you for your support to His house. Sometimes thanks does not seem to be enough. But we have a God who has a payoff for all of us.

Because we are our brother's keeper, we must pray daily for one another that the Lord will watch over us and keep us!

Saints, continue to fight the good fight of faith. Lay hold onto eternal life. Your best will get better, but your best is yet to come. Elder Russell says that the steps of a good man and a good woman have been ordered by the Lord!

UPON THIS ROCK

(In Memory of Our Founder, Mother Josephine Stewart)

God bless you people of the most high God for your faithfulness to our Lord and Savior Jesus Christ, and your love for the household of faith. Saints, always keep Jesus on your mind. We have an obligation to serve the Lord and love the Lord with all that is within us; because He loved us first.

As I reflect and remember Mother Josephine Stewart, the Founder of Zion where I serve as the pastor, I recall that one of the scriptures she would say no matter what message she was bringing forth was, "For God so loved the world that He gave His only begotten Son, that whosoever believeth in him should not perish but have everlasting life." She would always tell us what Jesus told Peter, "...upon this Rock I will build my church; and the gates of Hell shall not prevail against it."

You see Saints that upon each of us Christ is building His church. The Word is building us up every day, and when we come together, Hell cannot conform us. All we have to do is stay in the race until our day is done.

Saints fight on. Keep your faith in Jesus Christ. The Word will help us stand in the evil day. We are in a world where demonic forces are present. But know that God through Jesus Christ our Lord, will allow us to walk through here with victory. God bless you all for your prayers. All of us need· prayer.

Remember to love one another, pray for one another, to fight the good fight of faith, and to lay hold onto eternal life. Elder Russell says that the steps of a good man and a good woman have been ordered by the Lord! Saints, we have better days ahead, even our best days will get better, but the very best is yet to come!

HAPPY RESURRECTION SUNDAY

Praise the Lord people of the most high God. The Lord Jesus Christ died for our sins and rose with our victory! Once again, we offer praise and thanksgiving to our one and only Deliverer.

Saints, our Lord created the heavens and the earth; not one thing was made without Him. Out of everything He made, we were His greatest creation. He made us out of His own image, His own likeness. After He finished all of His work, He inspected it and declared it was good!

Saints, this is the season we celebrate the death, burial and resurrection of our mighty conqueror. After power was transferred in the garden, we were under the power of darkness and in the hands of a wicked devil. But at Calvary, Jesus paid it all. He paid our penalty, took our sins, died on the cross and rose again with all power in Heaven and on Earth. The good news is God sent His Son and His Son gave His life. Now Christ is on the inside of every believer, and He is the hope of glory. So celebrate Saints. Our King is alive, He is well and so are we. I would encourage you to continue to look to the hills where our help cometh from the Lord. Rejoice, and again I say rejoice!

Don't stop your work. Work while it is day for when night comes, no one can work. So, work while it's day in your life.

Saints, fight the good fight of faith and lay hold onto eternal life. For the best will get better and your best is yet to come. Elder Russell says the steps of a good man and a good woman, have been ordered by the Lord!

FINISHED WORK

God bless you people of God. Once again the Lord has blessed us to see another day. We need to thank Him for His mercy and His goodness. If we don't give Him His praise, the rocks will cry out. Everything He does for us is great!

Saints, we are in a season where our pure minds can be refreshed again and again concerning our Lord and Savior, Jesus Christ. When the Christ child was born it was the beginning of a "finished work." Everything that belongs to our life and our godliness is finished. The power of godliness and the kingdom that ruled up until Jesus' birth, Jesus' death and Jesus' return is finished! Our struggle now is to believe, to keep the faith, to always fight the good fight of faith because Jesus was wounded and He was bruised. He was tormented and was born to be tormented for our sins, transgressions, and iniquities.

That is the reality, it was to set us free from our sins! So in this season when you sing a song, when you see the cross, to every believer it symbolizes our freedom. We were given the greatest gift in the world. Our salvation has been signed, sealed, and delivered by Jesus Christ our Lord. In this coming year, remember what you are going through has already been finished. Every test, trial and tribulation has been finished. Every scripture in the Bible points to "it is finished."

It was the birth of Jesus Christ that made Satan and every demon tremble. Satan knew it would be a showdown and the battle is won!

Thank you all for your work in the church-house. Whatever your task, assignment, or just showing up. God is going to bless the "faithful."
So Saints continue to fight the good fight of faith and lay hold onto eternal life. For your best will get better and your best is yet to come. Elder Russell says yes, the steps of a good man and a good woman, have been ordered by the Lord!

ON ASSIGNMENT!

"For what is a man profited, if he shall gain the whole world, and lose his own soul? Or what shall a man give in exchange for his soul? (St. Matthew 16:26)

We must stay focused and avoid distractions. Don't miss your "appointed" assignment because of unwillingness to give up those things not appointed by our Lord and Savior. God will assign us what to do. Don't take your eye off of your assignment for one second.

Obedience, faithfulness, and intimacy with the Lord are required. We must see the whole picture. What God ordains, He will maintain!

Keep the faith. Keep serving God because it is our faith that will make us whole!

Saints remember we haven't arrived yet, but we are on our way. We are closer than we want to believe.

Continue to fight the good fight of faith. Lay hold onto eternal life. Your best will get better, but your best is yet to come. Elder Russell reminds us that the steps of every good man and every good woman have been ordered by the Lord! "

STOP, LOOK AND LISTEN!

Saints, let the peace and joy of the Holy Ghost always be with you. Jesus said He would leave His peace with us always, and it is peace that passes all understanding. The calmness that we have in Christ is even greater than we could ever imagine.

People of the most high God, Stop, look and listen; It's time for us to draw closer to our heavenly Father. He's calling us to totally surrender to Him. He's been so merciful to let us see another day and have another chance and opportunity to love the Lord Jesus Christ with all of our hearts, souls, and minds. We need to stop and see the changing of time and see that everything in the earth has a season. When we stop to consider there is a time to be born, a time to pass away and that we will spend eternity someplace; either Heaven or Hell. That should be enough to make us better people. So while we're here enjoying our life in Christ, we should look around to see just how blessed we are. God made provisions for us to come to Him through Jesus Christ our Lord. What more can He do? If we close our hearts and minds to Him who called us to virtue and honor, where will we end up without Jesus in our lives?

Listen and let me tell you something. We are people of destiny. We have all been destined for greatness, but many won't fulfill their destiny because they were stopped by the devil. If by chance the devil has gotten the best of you, knocked you out and it seems like you just can't make it through your struggle, you need to get on your knees and call on Jesus. He'll come see about you. He'll revive you and restore your strength. We must be determined to live for God regardless of our tests and trials, because one day for sure we're going to meet Him, and we want it to be well with our soul.

God bless you Saints. Continue to pray for each other because each and every one of us needs prayer. People of God, labor while its day; when night comes all of our work ceases.

Fight the good fight pf faith. Lay hold on to eternal life. Your best will get better, but your very best is yet to come. Elder Russell put it in our hearts that our good steps have been ordered by the Lord!

SOME WILL, SOME WON'T – WHAT WILL YOU DO?

Saints, greetings in the name of our Lord and Saviour, Jesus Christ. We are His people and the sheep of His pasture and we are still holding a true testimony that our Lord is Lord of Lords and King of Kings. I bring you words of encouragement that a crown has been laid up for you by the Righteous Judge. He laid it up for all of those who love Him; Since we have been called according to His purpose and have been given an assignment to live for Him, we can claim our crown and have no regrets of ever accepting Jesus as our Lord and Saviour.

Saints, during this season of celebrating the birth of our Lord and Saviour, let us remember we're celebrating the fact that there was a birth, indeed. In all your shopping and preparing for the holiday, remember Jesus is the reason for the season. There would be no possible shedding of Jesus' blood if He hadn't been born. As the calendar is winding down and we are coming to a close of this year, remember the Lord wants us to remain faithful because He is faithful to us and His love is unconditional, but our destiny is conditional. The condition is confessing Him as Lord and Saviour and believing that Christ died and rose again for our salvation!

Saints, remember to pray for our bereaved families. Don't forget to pray for one another.

Continue to fight the good fight of faith, and lay hold onto eternal life, for your best will get better, but your very best is yet to come! Elder Russell says, our steps have been ordered by the Lord!

GOD DOES NOT CHANGE, BUT HE CHANGES US!

Saints of the most high God, we can take great confidence and assurance that our heavenly Father knows what is best for us. If we can place it in our hearts to get in line and get in step with

His plans and purpose, there would be no stopping us, His Christian 'army. The enemy purposely tries to keep us blind by telling us that God didn't say what He means or mean what He said. I remind you to never forget that we must keep an ear to hear what the Holy Spirit is saying to the church. For every situation that could arise to take our victory, Jesus was manifested to destroy those works.

The preaching and teaching of the Gospel is to keep us equipped and empowered; saturated in wisdom and knowledge of our heritage and covenant in Christ Jesus. Our heritage has made us rich and it has made us overcomers. Our covenant has been sealed by the blood of Jesus and every promise in the book is ours.

Saints, our Heavenly Father loved us so much that while we were yet sinners and sinning, He sent Jesus Christ to die on the cross. God saw the fiery pit that we were headed for that is a penalty for sin. Without a deliverer to stand in our place, we would be doomed. Our Father, in His great mercy and great love sent us Jesus Christ to save us. So, don't give up; the way is paved. The price was paid.

Keep looking up Saints, because He is always looking down on us. Don't forget to pray for one another. Let your faith cause you to look again and don't stop until your mission is accomplished.

Continue to fight the good fight of faith. Lay hold onto eternal life, for your best will get better, but your very best is yet to come! Elder Russell says, our good steps have been ordered by the Lord!

YOU HAVE SET YOURSELF UP FOR A BLESSING

Saints, I thank God for your love. My prayer is that the body of Christ, the saints of God, would manifest the fruit of the Spirit which exemplifies the perfect love of Christ, that we LOVE ONE ANOTHER. "For the "fruit of the Spirit is love, joy, peace, longsuffering, gentleness, goodness, faith, meekness, and temperance: against such there is no law. If we live in the spirit, let us also walk in the spirit." Galatians 5:22-23

We are going somewhere, we are headed somewhere; but we are headed nowhere without the fruit of the Spirit of the living God.

I often tell my church, "I thank you for your finances, I thank you for your prayers; but, if you really want to make me happier than the above, let the words I have preached and talked get in your spirit and make a radical change! If you really want to pattern yourself after Jesus, do what I also try every day to do – love everybody without dissimilation or discrimination!"

We are all God's children. Everyone is subject to change. Where there is life, there is hope. Get up now and be about your Father's concerns!

Fight the good fight of faith and lay hold onto eternal life. Your best will get better, and your best is yet to come. As Elder always says, the steps of a good man and a good woman have been ordered by the Lord!

NOW FAITH

God bless you Saints. The Lord has given us some good news. This good news disarms the support of bad news. Standing on the good news is the Word of God that supports us as we stand on faith. Our faith is now!

Saints, fear, uncertainty, grief, and tribulations are things that try to disarm us of our faith. The Lord reminds us that NOW faith will bring substance to our faith. Just keep believing, keep watching, stay in great expectations and keep this song in your heart, "How Great is our God!"

The Lord is looking for and seeking the men and women that will come back and say, "I believe you."

If for some reason you bend, you will not break because your faith plants you by the river of waters and reminds you how great is our God. Saints, use your weapons of prayer. We need each other's prayers.

Keep fighting the good fight of faith, lay hold onto eternal life, for your best will get better, but your very best is yet to come! Elder Russell says, "The steps of a good man and a good woman have been ordered by the Lord!"

PRESS FORWARD

God bless you Saints. Although Satan fights us, the Lord is in the background telling us to go ahead. If we do what He says, we come out victorious every time. Can you see that sometimes we walk by blind faith? If we can't see it but believe, God brings it to pass. We must keep the faith!

Saints don't forget, God does what God does. He will never leave us or forsake us. We just have to know what God does. We must understand the God we serve. We have to know that He is not against us, He is for us!

Saints, keep fighting the good fight of faith. Lay hold onto eternal life, for your best will get better, but your very best is yet to come! Elder Russell says, "Remember the steps of a good man and a good woman have been ordered by the Lord!"

YOU MUST BELIEVE AND SPEAK NOW

Praise the Lord people of God. It is a good thing to give praise to the Most High. Once again, I am writing to remind everyone, when you accept Jesus Christ, our Lord, our Redeemer, our Forgiver, our Healer, every transgression, every iniquity, and all peace is restored. It all took place at Calvary, God sent His Son, His Son gave His life for every sinner, our salvation, our eternal life. It's for all of us who will believe and receive. When Jesus Christ comes in, He brings eternal life. It's in the Son our Saviour.

People of God, our God is from everlasting to everlasting, there is no defeat in Him, in Him we live, we move, we have our being; and we are not defeated no matter what the test, no matter what comes our way, we have the power of life and death in our tongue, in our speaking, in our believing. Declare what God in the name of Jesus declares about His children. We are more than conquerors through Him that loves us. All we have to do is believe and speak to the mountain, then speak to our Lord and thank Him for the power that's in His Word to speak His Word over every circumstance in our lives. He did say we would have sickness that would try to attach itself to us, but He has given us power to speak to it – to the root and give God praise for victory. I am Pastor Russell and I approve this message.

Now fight the "good fight of faith. Lay Hold on to Eternal Life. Speak what Jesus spoke. Jesus said

He already prayed for us that our FAITH would not fail. So, get to speaking, get to dancing, LIVE for Jesus, and you will have JOY. Our best will get better but our very best is yet to come.

Elder Russell said to tell you our good steps have been ordered by the Lord.

WHAT A MIGHTY GOD WE SERVE!

Saints of the most high God, the Lord continues to watch over us and keep us. Our Father, in the name of Jesus Christ, always keeps doing great things for His children. He always sends His Word to tell us to knock, seek, and ask. If for any reason you have become discouraged, just take a look and see what the Lord has already done. We are on this earth another day to show forth the praises of Him that has brought us out of darkness into His marvelous light.

People of God, go to that secret place and call on Jesus. He will reveal himself to you, He will touch you, and He will deliver you. If you don't call Him, how will He hear you? So, call Him. He is your Father!

People of God, fight the good fight of faith; lay hold on eternal life. Your best will get better but your very best is yet to come. Elder Russell said your good Steps have been ordered by the Lord.

LOVE YOUR LIFE IN JESUS CHRIST

People of God, People of the most high God, Once again this is the day the Lord has made, we will rejoice and be glad in it!

We have been given everything that pertains to life and godliness. Everything means everything, Our Father took care of us at Calvary's Cross. Our Father sent His Son born of woman with flesh and blood. Every pain we feel, Jesus felt, every sickness, every sin, every disease, God sent Jesus to bear it in His body, to shed His precious blood to pay the penalty for our sins. Sin separated us from our heavenly Father. The blood of bulls, goats, turtle doves and any other sacrifice was not enough. It took the blood of a sinless Jesus, to become sin, to subject Himself to a death by laying down His life so humanity could be free from damnation and a devil's Hell. JESUS PAID THE PRICE for OUR REDEMPTION at CALVARY's CROSS!

Serving and believing Jesus Christ will bring us back into fellowship with our God. The death, burial and resurrection of Jesus gave us a door. We have been allowed back into fellowship with our Father. Jesus took the keys Satan had to bind and condemn us to Hell, but Jesus paid the price, took back the keys, which is authority, from Satan and gave us everything that pertains to Life and godliness in this earth.

So fight the "good fight of faith." Lay hold onto eternal life. Get close to our Lord. Love what He loves, hate what He hates; hate evil, pride, arrogancy, the evil way, and the froward mouth – which means contrary, not easily managed, says things displeasing to God, stubborn, and disobedient. These things God's People must get victory over, because Satan uses these things to open a door of ungodliness. Our best will get better but our very best is yet to come. Elder Russell says our good steps have been ordered by the Lord.

JESUS PAID THE PRICE

God Bless you People of God, saved by the Blood of Jesus, delivered by His power, set free by His death, burial and resurrection. We are His people who know without a doubt – JESUS is the very expression of God born of Virgin Mary. Our God put on a body, became a Son without sin to die for a sinful world, on a cruel cross.

Saints, we praise God in the name of Jesus Christ for every sacrifice He made. He did it all for us. Told us to love the Lord our God with all our heart, soul, body and to love one another.

Saints, don't you get it? We don't have time to waste. We have been given time and opportunity to serve the Lord and draw closer and tell somebody about a saving Jesus, a delivering Jesus, a healing Jesus! Wake up, get up, stand up, look up and see the salvation of the Lord. Our redemption is drawing near!

Fight the good fight of faith. Lay hold on eternal life. Our best will get better, but our very best is yet to come. Elder Russell says the steps of a good man and a good woman are ordered by the Lord.

ORDER OUR STEPS IN YOUR WORD!

Praise the Lord Saints! These few words are to encourage you to continue. To continue is to endure until the end. We have a race to run and whatever comes our way, we must glorify our Lord and Saviour, Jesus Christ.

Saints, with every new day we rise with a heart of thanksgiving, let's ask for guidance, ask for protection, and walk as children of the King: as lights in this dark world. Let not the weak who walk in darkness persuade us to be partakers of their evil deeds. We represent the kingdom of light, and we must walk in the light as Jesus declared, He is the Light of the World.

We praise the Lord for the month of October, Ministers Appreciation Month. We thank God for the ministers. The Word given in the house of God makes us all carriers of the Word. This is why we must hide the Word of God in our hearts, so we won't sin against God. You must see how important you and I are to the Lord. We must study to show the world there is a better way, and the better way is Jesus Christ.

So people of God, fight the good fight of faith. Lay hold on to eternal life. Your best will get better but your very best is yet to come. Elder Russell says our Good Steps have been ordered by the Lord.

WORK WHILE IT'S DAY IN YOUR LIFE!

People of God, this note is just a reminder that the time is here. The Lord is pouring his Spirit out on all flesh, the latter-day rain is falling; don't miss out on the renewing - be filled with the Spirit of the Living God. The Spirit in you is the hope of Glory. We the people of Almighty God have been given power, soundness of mind, power that brings healing to our bodies, healing to others and to walk and live for Jesus which is a mission each child of God must be on in Jesus' name.

Read your Bible without stopping. You are walking with the Word. Anytime you feel out of your steadfastness, the Word inside will strengthen you. The Word will not change. The things JESUS said will not fail, and you will not fail. Stay in love with your heavenly Father; always seek Him, always talk to Him, and listen. He will speak back.

Satan wants our ear to tell us our Father doesn't care and that our God will never answer, but Satan is a liar! Jesus promised us He has come that we might have life and life more abundantly. We get in trouble when we walk the way of flesh, when we overlook God's Word and

His will. Our God in the name of Jesus will never leave us. Jesus doesn't want our everyday to be spent seeing what He didn't do. He is doing great things. The Lord gives peace to His children no matter what the test is. The problem is, our test will not last forever, we are to bless the Lord at all times. Be still and know your God. Surely you must stay connected. No matter who doesn't praise Him, don't you stop.

Saints, fight the good fight of faith. Lay hold on to eternal life. Your best will get better but your very best is yet to come. Elder Russell says our Good Steps have been ordered by the Lord!

HIDE US JESUS!

God bless you people of God. The Lord has kept us by His mercy and His grace for us. In the name of Jesus, we give Him praise for this.

People of God, be strong in the Lord. This is not the time to be weak as evil times rapidly come upon us. Every child of God should pray more, praise more, worship more, and for our sake, forgive more so we can love more!

Our Lord is sending His Word every day to our hearts. The Word of God is a strong tower. The righteous are always running to enter the Word of God that teaches us how to realize what is the mind and will of the Almighty God. We must walk according to His will and His way. As we study the Word, we will show ourselves approved as God's workers who will not be ashamed. We will be able to rightly divide the Word in the name of Jesus Christ, our Lord and Savior.

People of God, fight the good fight of faith; lay hold on to eternal life. Let nothing separate you from the Word and the will of God. Our best will get better, but our very best is yet to come. Continue to pray for each other. Elder Russell said our good steps are ordered by the Lord. Pray one for another, that ye may be healed.

OUR GOD, OUR DELIVERER!

God Bless you people of God. We are here today because of the mercy and grace of our Lord and Saviour, Jesus Christ. Each of us must realize how blessed our time on this earth is. We have had all of our sins forgiven, and all of our souls redeemed from the power of Satan.

We have received redemption through His blood; we ought to dedicate our lives to Jesus. To live for Him and live for Him until we die! The Word of God has made it plain. Without Jesus Christ, we have no life. The Spirit and power of God have made it possible for His children, His believers to successfully walk every day with victory. It is left up to each of us to hear His Word, understand His Word, and to obey His Word.

Elder Russell preached a message one Sunday telling us we must not be fearless but fear the Lord remembering Psalm 111:10. "The fear of the Lord is the beginning of wisdom; a good understanding have all they that do his commandments, his praise endureth forever."

People of God, fight the good fight of faith. Lay hold onto eternal life. Your best will get better, but your very best is yet to come. Elder Russell says our good steps have been ordered by the Lord.

PRAISE IS WHAT WE DO

People of God in the name of Jesus Christ our Lord and Saviour, our Lord has brought us again to today. Yesterday is gone. When tomorrow comes, it's another day; so bless the Lord every day and never let a day go by in your life on this earth without giving Glory to our God in Jesus' name.

People of God, sometimes we have to do like David and ask the Lord "What shall I do to overcome this problem?" or inquire how to get through another difficult time. People of God, we are more than conquerors, and our hearts can be strengthened by the fact that our God said He loved us so much that he laid down His life for us. No man has greater love than our Lord and Saviour Jesus Christ, we are better than blessed.

Saints, fight the good fight of faith. Lay hold onto eternal life. Your best will get better, but your very best is yet to come. Elder says the steps of a good man or woman are always ordered by the Lord!

WALK IN THE LIGHT

Praise the Lord people of the most high God, in the name of Jesus Christ our Lord and Saviour. Everyone who has made Jesus Lord of their life, is no longer walking in darkness. Light has come, and we must always remember to walk in the Light. Jesus is the Light of the world. Some refuse to walk in the Light. Some refuse to abide in the Light. This is written to believers. When believers think about the fact that in darkness the devil does his dirt, those who don't want to change, continue walking in darkness which is sin. Those who want to walk in the truth of God will continue to walk in the Word of God where the Light always shines.

People of God, in the name of Jesus, pray, sing, read, study and take every day to give thanks to the Lord, who calls His people to be overcomers. In Jesus, we have life. The life in Jesus brings Light.

God bless you People of God. Continue to press your way. Draw closer to God. When you don't know what to do, be still, Jesus will strengthen you on every side. Oh, how He loves His children. If you don't know JESUS, Receive

Jesus as your Lord and Saviour. Invite Him into your heart. Let Him forgive your sins, and then serve the Lord the rest of your life. The Lord will do you good. Heaven will be your home.

Saints of God, fight the "good fight of faith." Lay hold on to eternal life. Your best will get better, but your very best is yet to come. So, praise the Lord at all times! Elder Russell says, the steps of a good man and woman have been ordered by the Lord.

WORSHIP THE LORD

Praise the Lord people of God. bless His holy name. Our Lord has kept us. He has raised us once again for such a time as this; a time when we as people of the most high God must lift up a standard, let our lights shine, love as brethren, and pray for one another. We have been called out of darkness. These are the days when we have noticed there are changes in the atmosphere, and changes in the whole world. Our Lord is not leaving His church without knowledge and understanding of the times and seasons, we are living in.

People of God, know this! We are to be an army of believers that pray, fast, witness, and warn people to run for their lives. We who fear God and believe God, we know the Lord Our God, in the Name of Jesus, says what He means and means what He says. Jesus said His house must be a house of prayer. Many have made the house of God -seem like any other house, but it is not. The glory of the Lord is in His house. The sick run in to be healed. The weak come to be strengthened. The sinners come to find rest for their souls. My brothers and sisters, what are you looking for in the house of God? Weakness of others? Something to talk about? We come to His house to learn how to please the Almighty God in the name of Jesus Christ!

So Saints fight the good fight of faith. Lay hold onto eternal life. Your best will get better, but your very best is yet to come. Elder Russell says our steps have been ordered by the Lord.

P. S. Walk in the path of Righteousness.

RISE AND PUT ON STRENGTH

God bless you people of the most High God. We thank God for another day. He kept us yesterday. Today is a new day, with new opportunities and new chances to be stronger in the Lord today than we was yesterday. Today we must realize if it had not been for the Lord on our side, we would not be here today. He is always there with His finger of love that touched us and gave us another chance to lift Him up and another chance to let Him know that without Him we are nothing.

Oh, if we would praise the Lord for all He has done! We must rebuke the devil, send his demons out of our presence by rebuking them in the name of Jesus, and praising Our God for He is worthy. He is teaching us through His Word we have power over the power of the devil in the name of Jesus.

Saints of God, come into the Lord's presence with thanksgiving and praises, lifting Jesus up. We must have a personal walk with God. Many spirits of evil are sent from the devil to render us helpless and unfruitful, but Jesus died and rose again to save us and empower us. He rose up with all power. He promised us we too would have power after the Holy Ghost comes upon us.

Thank God He did not leave us powerless. He did not leave us alone. We are in a world that has been contaminated with sin. That's why the Lord has told us not to love the world or the things in the world. If we love the world, the love of the Father is not in us. Take inventory and begin to rise up in your faith in the name of Jesus. We have been given a name that's above every name.

Keep His name in your heart, soul and body, and fight the good fight of faith. Lay hold on to eternal life. Your best will get better, but your very best is yet to come. Elder Russell says our good steps have been ordered by the Lord.

OUR KING IS COMING

Praise the Lord, People of Almighty God, in the name of Jesus Christ Our Lord and Saviour. Once again, the Lord has smiled on us and blessed us to see another day and another opportunity to worship Him. Saints, the Kingdom of our God is an Everlasting Kingdom, and it continues throughout all generations.

People of God, we have sisters and brothers we don't know. They have met the Lord Jesus Christ and when the day, the gathering of all the children of the Kingdom comes, what a mighty reunion, both small and great it will be! We will be blessing the King of Kings and Lord of Lords, beholding the one who saved us, the one who promised the Church He was going away but He was coming back again. He said He would wipe all tears away.

Saints of God, our Father will reign forever and ever! Work, labor fast, pray, live holy, and most of all, stay in the Word of God and love one another, as we continue to love our Lord.

Saints the Lord Jesus laid down His life, shed His Blood, and gave us a right to eternal life. So continue to Fight the good fight of faith; lay hold onto eternal life, your best will get better, but your very best is yet to come, Our Lord IS coming back! Be glad He told you to come into the house of the Lord. Elder Russell reminds us, "Our steps" have been ordered by the Lord."

OUR SAVIOR LIVES

Saints we are so grateful to our Lord, for He has blessed us beyond measure. He is so good, kind and merciful, there is none like Our Lord. He keeps doing great things for the whole wide world.
    Some thank Him. Some don't. We are a people who know our Lord, and we keep the faith, through the good times and through the challenging times. We know that whatever comes our way, we are never abandoned, for we serve a God who Loves us with an everlasting love, He forgives our sins, He restores us over and over again.
    Saints, don't let the evil one deceive you to believe God is not a good God. The devil is a liar. Our Father loves us so much, He laid down His life for us. We give glory and honor to our Lord and Saviour, Jesus Christ. Our God put on flesh, walked this earth, redeemed us, and removed our transgressions from us.
    Saints, continue to fear the Lord reverently. Serve the Lord, Love the Lord out of a sincere heart, declare His name all the days of your life. We are blessed Forever.

Saints, continue to fight the good fight of faith; lay hold onto eternal life. Your best will get better, but your very best is yet to come!

JOY COMES IN THE MORNING

Praise the Lord, People of God, once again, we thank God for His protection, for His goodness, and for the love He has towards us. We thank God for times in our lives where He brought us through difficult moments and brought us through unseen dangers. Thank God we're still here to testify to the Greatness of our God.

People of God, we pray for daybreak. We know how Jacob felt wrestling with the Angel of the Lord until daybreak. In all our lives, daybreak comes when our joy comes back. Daybreak is when you realize the devil has been on your territory and you have been given strength from God to put him in his place. When we rise up knowing we have power over the power of the devil. That's DAYBREAK. The Lord prepares us every day to see His blessings. It is not how we start out, it's how we end.

Jesus taught His disciples how to pray. We too must pray. Prayer is the key that puts the devil in his place. When we believe for what we have prayed for, God will work everything out. Pray, because we always need a Word from the Lord. Prayer calms many storms. We have been called by Almighty God In the name of Jesus Christ, our Savior. God will bring us out so that we can tell somebody that our God will deliver. People of God; the Lord always brings us together to lift the name of Jesus, and to hear what the Spirit has to say to the Church.

Fight the good fight of faith. Lay hold onto eternal life. Your best will get better, but your very best is yet to come! Continue to pray one for another, as we see the day approaching. Elder Russell says the steps of a "Good man and woman" are ordered by the Lord.

NOW FAITH IS THE SUBSTANCE OF THINGS HOPED FOR

Praise the Lord, People of God. I want to remind you that blessings and miracles belong to the children of God. We must take it by faith and force. That means don't give in; don't give up that which is ours. By faith, we can have not only eternal life, but life in abundance which is claimed by our faith. Without faith, it is impossible to please God. So the words of this book are to encourage you to keep the faith.

People of God, we have an inheritance given to us by our heavenly Father, and we have been given a name which is above every name. We can call Him in distress, in sickness, physical or mental. The name of JESUS can move any demon. It's in the name Saints! So get busy and put the devil that's torturing you on the run. Turn the tables and torture him. The Name of JESUS has bought our Liberty! Remember Demas in the Bible. He went part of the way but did not finish because he loved this present world and would not continue. So take a lesson, hold to your faith and endure until the end. While you are enduring, sing a song, pray a prayer and praise your GOD.

Fight the good fight of faith. Lay hold onto eternal life. Your best will get better, but your very best is yet to come. He's on the way!! Elder Russell says the steps of a good man and a good woman are ordered by the Lord.

REMEMBER

Praise the Lord People of the most high God, in the name of Jesus Christ Our Lord and Saviour. I want to bring to your remembrance, the words of our Saviour Jesus in the book of Matthew. Jesus said, "If any many will come after me, let him deny himself, and take up his cross and follow me." Remember when the Chief Shepherd shall appear, we shall receive a crown of glory that will not fade away. In the book of Peter, our Lord said, "Casting all your care upon him because he Gareth for us."

People of God, Jesus said He is Alpha and Omega, the beginning and the end. He is first and last. Be still and know your God. Be still and know the Great Shepherd, the one who takes care of all our needs and wants. Bless the Lord at all times.

People of God, I give thanks for my church, New Zion Revival Temple, our Ministers, each member, every visitor, I thank God for His sanctuary, and His Word that's "a lamp unto our feet and a light to our path." God bless and keep all the Saints in His mighty Word is my prayer.

People of God, fight the "good fight of faith." Lay hold onto eternal life. Our best will get better, but our very best is yet to come. Elder Russell says our steps have been ordered by the Lord.

BUILD UPON THE ROCK

Praise the Lord, people of God, The Lord has kept us safe and back together to lift up the name of Jesus and to hear what the Spirit is saying to the Church. The Gospel of Jesus Christ is to show us, to teach us, to beg us and to persuade us to enter into His presence by His Word. Our Lord is faithful that promised in His Word to keep us, provide for us and let no devil separate us from Him when we abide in His Word. The Lord Jesus Christ has taken our troubles, as we give them to Him, one storm after another. He promised us according to Mark 4:35, "We are going to the other side."

We have the same key Jesus gave to Peter. That key is authority to use His name to bind and to loose while we are on this earth. The Lord has great things for everyone that will endure until the end. Jesus came to save His people from their sins. We are so blessed to be in His army and to bless His name. Our purpose on this earth is to work until our day is done. We must lift up the name of Jesus and let our light shine so that we can glorify our Father which art in Heaven.

Fight the "good fight of faith." Lay hold on to eternal life. Your best will get better, but your very best is yet to come! People of God, Elder Russell says, "The steps of a good man and woman are ordered by the Lord."

CHRIST IS THE ANSWER

God Bless you people of the most high Saviour, Jesus Christ, Our Lord. Saints, the Lord has brought us up to this day and given us another day to come together to lift up His name and to remind the devil it is our Lord Jesus Christ who died for us. He alone is worthy to be praised every day. Jesus is worthy to be lifted up every day. Without our Saviour, we would have no hope in this world; but because of Jesus we can lift up our heads and have hope. We can walk by faith in this world.

Sometimes in this life, looking at the happenings, it looks like all is lost. For the unbelievers it doesn't seem bright, but for the believers, the time is at hand. We have no time to waste. Believers know Jesus is the Light of the world, and people everywhere have begun to call and to serve Jesus. People everywhere have begun to lift up Holy hands. People everywhere are recognizing who the King of Glory is.

People of God, be strengthened in the Word. Jesus Christ said, "I'm going away, but I'm coming back again." Jesus said, "I will show my people great and mighty things."

People of God, fight the "good fight of faith." Lay hold onto eternal life. Our best will get better but our very best is yet to come. Elder Russell says our good steps have been ordered by the Lord.

JESUS IS TRUTH

Bless the Lord all His children. We are His people. We are His sheep. He is our Father and He is Worthy to be praised. We are the people of God, in the name of Jesus Christ, Our Lord and Saviour. We are supposed to be His witnesses in all the earth. We have been commissioned to let our lights shine in a dark world. We are the salt of the Earth. We make a difference. Our love for our Lord and each other will draw sinners to the cross.

Saints, it was at the cross that Jesus submitted to death for the sins of the world. It is Jesus who made it possible for us to be forgiven of our sins and to come out of every sinful sin. The devil tried to stop us with condemnation. He tried to convince us that Jesus doesn't love us, so we won't love Jesus. But we know Satan is a liar.

People of God, get right with God, and let nothing separate you from His great love.

Saints, fight the "good fight of faith." Lay hold onto eternal life. Our best will get better, but our very best is yet to come. Elder Russell reminds us, our steps have been ordered by the Lord.

GIVE GOD THE GLORY

Praise the Lord people of the King of kings and Lord of lords. How great it is to trust in God, in the name of Jesus Christ Our Lord and Saviour. This is a time in our lives when we must hold fast to our hope in the Lord. Our faith must stand fast. Our faith is an everlasting faith. We must hold to our Saviour and give God glory each and every day. Pray without ceasing, love and forgive every day, stay in the Word of God, lean not to our own understanding, but understand what the Word says. Always give Praise and glory to Almighty God in the name of JESUS.

Jesus Christ is our Lamb of God. He came to reconcile us back to God. Mankind lost fellowship in the Garden of Eden when the devil deceived man in the garden, and man believed the devil's lie. But through Jesus Christ, we are the people of God, who worship our Lord and Saviour and glorify God every day.

People of God, fight the "good fight of faith." Lay hold on to eternal life. Our best will get better but our very best is yet to come. God bless and keep each of us. Now run and tell somebody JESUS CHRIST Is the answer to all of our issues. Elder Russell says the steps of a good man and a good woman have been ordered by the Lord.

FAITH – USE WHAT YOU GOT

Praise God and God bless you, and Keep you is my prayer for you, at all times.

People of God, I know, no weapon that is formed against you will prosper. Just keep faith in Almighty God in the name of Jesus. For your faith will make you whole. Your faith will move mountains. Your faith will open closed doors. Your faith will make the impossible possible. There is nothing too hard for our Lord.

People of God, this book is to encourage you while you go through this life when things sometimes seem to work against the hope that we have. But Saints one thing is sure - there is hope and power in the name of Jesus Christ, Our Lord and Saviour.

Saints, read the Word of God. Keep your faith strong. Be wise – keep oil in your vessels. Never let what you have go lacking by not worshipping, not being obedient, walking after the flesh, or being more excited about the world than you are about Jesus Christ and the things of God. Wake up. Pray. Fast. See where you stopped having love for the Lord like you used to. Remember the Lord's arms are still outstretched. You still have time.

Fight the "good fight of faith." Lay hold onto eternal life. Your best will get better, but your very best is yet to come. Elder Russell says our good steps have been ordered by the Lord.

FROM EVERLASTING TO EVERLASTING

Praise the Lord people of the most high God. We thank Almighty God, in the name of Jesus Christ our Lord and Saviour, that He has allowed us to come together again to give Him praise for all the things He has done for us. If anyone ever asks you why we serve the Lord, tell them there are many reasons. Our main reason is we found a man who was able to set us free, bring peace to our dying souls, set us free from sin and death, keep us every day and forgive us from day to day offenses.

People of God our brother Paul on the road to torture and persecute the people of God for worshipping Jesus, had an encounter with the Lord. Jesus made Himself real to our brother Paul, ever since the day he met Jesus, he served Jesus. Paul was one of the greatest evangelists that lived. You and I can do the same thing. When we are saved, we become lights in the world leading people to the One who will deliver, love and set them free. Because we know from everlasting to everlasting, our Lord is Lord and King of all mankind. That's why we can fast, pray and plead for sinners everywhere. Because we know Jesus will set His people free!

Saints, fight the "Good fight of faith." Lay hold on eternal life. Our best will get better but our very best is yet to come. Elder Russell says our good steps have been ordered by the Lord.

PRAISE YE THE LORD

Praise the Lord people of Almighty God. Our Father has brought us together once again. We give Him praise and honor. What a wonderful Saviour. Everybody ought to know this great Redeemer. He has made provisions for every human being to make it into the Kingdom of Heaven. Heaven is a place that when we get there, nobody can put us out. It is the devil who has tried to keep us from making it to Heaven.

Psalms 98:4 says "Make a joyful noise unto the Lord all the earth: make a loud noise, rejoice, and sing praises." People, our Lord is worthy.

Build yourself up on your most holy faith. Whatever you need, believe God and ask, trust and believe.

Saints, we are in a season of refreshing. This refreshing comes from the Lord. We as children of God must draw closer. We must call on the name of Jesus hard and without ceasing. Call Him in your heart, with your mouth, in your spirit, and let go and let God have His way. Keep oil in your vessel. Don't let your light go out. If you think you are weak, if you feel you are not as strong as you want to be, now is the time {the acceptable time) to call on Jesus; He is just a prayer away.

Saints, draw closer to Christ Jesus. He is the only one who can give us strength to survive in this world and in the world to come. Eternal life Is ours. Don't let another day go by without Jesus.

Saints, fight the "Good fight of faith." Lay hold on eternal life. Our best will get better but our very best is yet to come. Elder Russell says, our good steps have been ordered by the LORD.

SERVE THE LORD ALWAYS

Praise the Lord Saints. Bless the Lord at all times. Let His praises continue to be in your mouth. Thank the Lord. He chose us in Him to be holy, righteous and without blame before Him in love.

Please your Saviour and be forever grateful. We would not be where we are if it had not been for Him. Thank our Father who gave us a chance to accept Him, and we said "yes" to the Lord and His heavenly calling.

Saints be of good courage, no matter how difficult, how trials come on every hand, the Lord always brings us out on time. What a mighty God we serve.

So Saints take every moment and have a heart of thanksgiving. Our Father will send peace in the midst of every storm. Saints have faith in God. He promised to never leave us or forsake us. We are blessed. We are better than blessed.

Saints, fight the "good fight of faith." Lay hold onto eternal life, our best will get better, but our very best is yet to come. Elder Russell says, to remind everyone, the steps of a good man and a good woman are ordered by the Lord.

THE BLOOD

May the grace of Almighty God be with us each day of our lives.

My prayer is that God's anointing rest upon us, keep us, teach us and never let us forget the purpose of Jesus Christ going to Calvary's cross and what he accomplished when he took our sins upon himself and died on a cruel lonely cross. He was buried, and He rose again. It was at the cross that Jesus Christ shed His Blood, bought pardon, and gave each of us - every man, woman, and child born in this sinful world, a right to the tree of life, that we were entitled to from creation. All mankind has to do is receive JESUS CHRIST as our Saviour and Lord, live for Him, and serve Him. We then become partakers of eternal life. This is available to all who receive JESUS and understand that He took our sins and shed His blood to set us free from everlasting damnation.

People of God, what a friend we have in JESUS, our Lord, Our Saviour, our Deliverer, and our Redeemer; and don't forget He's coming back again to receive His children, and He is going to take every believer, whether dead or alive, back with Him when he comes back. Just Be Ready!

So fight the "good fight of faith." Lay hold onto eternal life. Our best will get better, but our very best is yet to come. Elder Russell says, the steps of a good man and a good woman are ordered by the Lord. We thank our Lord for his precious BLOOD.

GET READY...BE READY...STAY READY

Praise the Lord, people of the most high God. We are God's people in the name of Jesus Christ our Lord. Not only are we His people, but we are blessed and highly favored. We are called His friends. We are His redeemed. We are the Bride waiting for the Bridegroom. Our redemption is very near.

People of God, since we know what's happening in the world, our faith should be increased day by day. We should be in the Word and constantly in prayer. Whether we have twenty, thirty, or fifty years on this earth, every day we are given, we should be living and pressing towards the place. When the Lord does come, we should be living, waiting, watching and in great expectation.

People of God, all Christians are lights in this dark world, examples to our families and friends. Our message is Jesus Christ died to give all of us eternal life – life everlasting!

So people of God, fight the "good fight of faith." Lay hold onto eternal life. Our best will get better, but our very best is yet to come. Elder Russell says, the steps of a good man and a good woman are ordered by the Lord.

BY HIS STRIPES, I AM HEALED

Praise the Lord, people God. It's another day the Lord has brought us and kept us. He has always been a faithful God. People of God, in every situation, even in sickness and in every time when we feel alone, our Lord is right there. He is our healer. He is our deliverer. Many times, the Lord commands us to be still. This battle belongs to our heavenly Father; So while we keep looking to the hills, our Father is working this out.

Saints, by every Word that proceeds out of the mouth of our God, He will back up every word, all He wants us to do is to have faith and believe what the Lord said He will perform. Saints, let the words from your mouth always be, "I believe God." By His stripes we are already healed!

Saints, fight the "good fight of faith." Lay hold onto eternal life. Your best will get better, but your very best is yet to come. Elder Russell says, our good steps have been ordered by the Lord.

A MESSAGE FROM THE SAINTS OF NEW ZION

(A Message To Our Pastor and Elder)

"For the vision is yet for an appointed time..."

We thank God for our precious Pastor & for Elder Russell.

The Saints of New Zion earnestly and eagerly await the words from the Lord given to Pastor.
We all have been guided in numerous ways with your reminders that our "walk of faith" is pleasing to our heavenly Father; that some hear but cannot profit because it is not mixed with FAITH, and when we mix the words sent to us with FAITH and put them into action, which is to believe, we will be blessed and highly favored!

We will continue to. fight the good fight of faith; lay hold onto eternal life for our best will get better and our very best is yet to come. As Elder reminds us, "The steps of a good man and a good woman have been ordered by the Lord"

THIS IS WHY! – TO YOU ALL

To my family, all of the New Zion Revival Temple Church family, friends and saints of the most high God; To each minister, deacon, missionary, each and every ordinary person who loves the Lord, Jesus Christ, who has taken up their cross, and followed Him and learned of Him:

We have learned that Jesus loved the whole human race. He loved us when we were worthless losers, without God and abusing ourselves. One day there was a knock on the door of our heart, and we opened the door and let Jesus in. The one we let in was the one who died so we could see our self-worth. We let in the one who took our place on Calvary. He pardoned our sins. He made us kings and priests. Every time I look around there is someone else to tell of the love of Jesus. There is someone else to pull up out of despair; there is another opportunity to let some fallen soul know Jesus will pardon you and forgive you. But most of all to teach others to go and spread the good news. This is why, people of God, because we are the bride of Christ, we are going to live with Him for ever and ever.

If I have made your life better by, preaching and teaching the Gospel or by being an ear, or by trying to comfort you in your time of sorrow, and if for any reason God has allowed my life to touch yours in any way, to God.be the Glory.

God has given me a special love and a deep concern for each of you. It has been a pleasure to love you, to serve you. and most of all to prepare you. I thank God for using an ordinary person like myself to lead a great army like you and to speak into your lives. This is why I continue. You are the reason!

Saints, please remember one another in prayer and continue to fight the good fight of faith; lay hold on to eternal life for your best will get better and your very best is yet to come. Elder Russell says the steps of a good man and a good woman have been ordered by the Lord!

Love, Elder & Pastor Russell
Pray for one another!

ABOUT THE AUTHOR

Pastor Deloise Russell is an author, artist, poet, matriarch, wife, pastor and a child of God. She has been the pastor of the New Zion Revival Temple Church for 39 years. She is the wife of Elder Brad Russell who is a major, anointed part of her life and ministry and who serves as head of the Men's Ministry at New Zion.

Pastor Deloise Russell is a woman of love and great compassion. Her motherly love is felt by all of her congregation and anyone she meets. One of her passions is to minister to women that are or have been incarcerated. One of her goals is to build a home for women that have been recently released from incarceration.

Pastor Russell was born in Suffolk, Virginia. She has loved God since she was a little girl and always knew that He had a plan for her life. The full story of her life is too immense to put in the back of this book. That's why she has plans to write another book about her life story. She also has plans to write a book of poetry.

Pastor Russell is excited about her future and what God has in store for her!

ORDER INFORMATION

You can order additional copies of

God's Hand Is Still Outstretched

at Amazon.com, BN.com
Kindle Books on Amazon and your local bookstores (By Request)

Please leave a review for this book on Amazon and let other readers know how much you enjoyed reading it.

Thank you!

www.ingramcontent.com/pod-product-compliance
Lightning Source LLC
Chambersburg PA
CBHW070814100426
42742CB00012B/2358